HOW TO MAKE A LIVING in the COUNTRY

How To Make A Living in the Country

WILLIAM E. OSGOOD

Charlotte, Vermont
GARDEN WAY PUBLISHING 1974

Library of Congress Catalog Card Number: 73-89131
ISBN (Paper) 0-88266-021-7
ISBN (Casebound) 0-88266-022-5

COPYRIGHT 1974 BY GARDEN WAY PUBLISHING CO.
DESIGNED BY CYNDY M. BRADY
PRINTED IN THE UNITED STATES OF AMERICA

"If a man has good corn, or wood, or boards, or pigs to sell, or can make better chairs or knives, crucibles or church organs than anybody else, you will find a broad, hardbeaten path to his house, though it be in the woods."

Ralph Waldo Emerson

ILLUSTRATED BY MARLENE FRENCH RUSSELL

Contents

Preface

In 1970 a Gallup poll revealed that six out of every ten residents of urban areas would move out of the city if they could undertake to make a living in the country. The grime and filth of city life is clearly present to the respondents of this survey, but whether they are seriously interested in country life I think is an open question. Perhaps it is a wish to get away from an increasingly intolerable situation, more than actively to seek country life.

I consider myself to be a countryman, with no reservations. Although I'm not poor, I do lead rather an austere life and so does my family. So I really wonder how many of the sixty per cent of the city folks in the Gallup poll *really* want to exchange their way of life for something like mine or for the life styles of others that you will read about in these pages. There is no doubt, however, that a significant number of people *are* thinking rather seriously about trying to make a living in the country, and it is to these people that this book is addressed. If you are one, I hope you will get some satisfaction, pleasure, and profit from reading what is here.

HOW TO MAKE A LIVING IN THE COUNTRY is based to a considerable degree on the results of questionnaires sent to a number of people who actually have moved to the country. In addition, others who have been quite successful in their country-based enterprises have been interviewed, and I have supplemented their experience with reminiscences of my own, while much of the basic research for this book was done by Evelyn V. Loveday. In the process of preparing the manuscript I am everlastingly indebted to the wisdom and good thinking of many others, but I can't call any of these people to task for omissions or misinterpretations. That responsibility must rest with me.

As an introduction to the sort of thing I have in mind, read this story of Ed and Sue Jarvis who are in their early thirties and have two children.

Ed has been employed by Metabolic Processes, Inc., as an accountant. He has been with them since graduation from high school, except for some time spent in the Army, and has worked his way to the top of his pay scale. Further advancement with the firm is not open to him because he lacks a college education. Right now he is rather frustrated in his work because of its routine nature and because there is no further opportunity to get ahead.

While Ed has always lived in the city, Sue was brought up on a large midwestern farm. She misses the open country and has wanted to get out of the city. Her enthusiasm for rural life has rubbed off on Ed, and the two children also have enjoyed country vacations immensely.

Metabolic Processes is a large drug manufacturer. Although Ed is in the accounting department, he has become interested in drugs themselves and especially in the so-called medicinal herbs. He takes home books from the company research library and he and Sue study them. He also talks with the men in the research and development laboratories. Both Ed and Sue have become fascinated with herbal medicine and they often talk about it around the supper table with their children.

Finally they have come to the conclusion that they may as well get out of the city altogether and move to the country where they can grow some of these herbs on a commercial basis. But since trying to grow and sell them is a risky venture and will take some time to get established, Ed will continue to use his skill as an accountant, working part-time for small businesses and individuals, doing tax returns and other such jobs. Sue, who has experience in gardening, will undertake to get the herb business started. The children will help their mother in spare time from school. Then, as the herb business expands, Ed can devote more of his time to that.

They did make the move to the country and got the herb business started, but they found their markets were limited and didn't provide enough income. They learned about the need for

laboratory animals and thus supplemented the income from herbs and Ed's accounting practice with the sale of rabbits, for which there is a great demand at Ed's old place of employment.

Later, by the time the children reached college age, the Jarvises were well established in the medicinal herb business. The family has sufficient income from this business to help with college expenses, and with the increased demand for medicinal herbs, they are well on their way to making this a primary source of income. Ed gradually is phasing out his accounting practice and devotes most of his time to working with Sue in their own business.

Ed and Sue Jarvis don't really exist. I have made them up out of many of the details that have gone into the preparation of this book. Their story is the point where fiction ends and fact begins, for the rest of the book represents real life experience.

HOW TO MAKE A LIVING IN THE COUNTRY really is a guidebook to show people the various and also sometimes complicated routes used by others in getting established in a new way of life away from the metropolis, or methods used by country folk so they don't have to move to the city.

For those who want to quit urban living, be advised that changing a life style is not an easy matter. It takes a good deal of venturesomeness and self-discipline. But if you are a person who truly wishes to take a firm grip on the steering wheel and turn off the smog-shrouded eight-lane freeways, perhaps the advice in this book can guide you past the more disappointing routes and lead you to a realm of satisfaction.

Part I

The Ingredients

For a little less than a year my wife, young daughter, and I lived in a large city while I was attending graduate school. That was enough for us, and we were most anxious to get out. While living in the city wasn't exactly a nightmare, it was pretty close to it, and it re-doubled my love for rural landscapes where I was brought up. My wife, on the other hand, was brought up in the suburbs of a large city but had spent many pleasant summers in the mountains of New England, so she had a taste for country life, too. Although she is not such a monomaniac about country living as I, she really appreciates the peace and quiet of the countryside or the comparative simplicity of village life.

What do we think of as the "country" in the U.S.A. and Canada? Farmland and forest obviously is rural and needs no qualifications, but we would enlarge the scope of this somewhat and include in our definition the many villages and towns and the fringe areas of cities having populations up to about 50,000. To clarify this even more, let me say that all orientations are distant from anything that can be called a metropolitan area.

The metropolis or city state from ancient Grecian times seems to have had much in its favor. But nowadays the metropolis as we see it is a vastly obese and sickening example of social breakdown. Moreover, we have at hand also the super-metropolis, sometimes referred to as Megalopolis. It's a current term referring to a conglomeration of cities that have oozed together to make up a continuous urban complex, an example being the eastern seaboard of the U.S.A. extending from Arlington, Virginia, northwards to Nashua, New Hampshire. Another example might be the region of the St. Lawrence River valley downstream from Montreal almost to Quebec City. The West Coast of the U.S.A.

could provide other examples and, if that weren't enough, I could take you overseas to the Netherlands and Great Britain.

But really if you are reading this book you are not much interested in references to city life, and I mention it only as a means of contrast to the sort of living to be discussed at greater length.

For my own definition, I say that a country house should be out of sight of neighbors, except in wintertime when the leaves are off the trees. Others will have their own qualifications, and more generally speaking, a country place is where there is a considerable amount of greenery in view, either trees or grass, and the asphalt jungle is remote. Then, with these pronouncements about what constitutes the "country," let's look into the situation of making a living there.

Making a "Living"

When some friends heard that I was writing about making a living in the country, they concluded that I had found a magic formula to make the economics of country life painless and easy. I had to disappoint them, just as you will be, if you're looking for the primrose path to everlasting bliss, for my own forty-six years of country life combined with an aggregate of a couple hundred years of experience (of those who have cooperated in the preparation of this book) still don't provide any panaceas.

From my own point of view (and I think this is quite generally shared by other country folk), it's the intangibles we seek in country living, not a fat bank account nor having hundreds of people at our beck and call.

Intangibles

To summarize these things, let me review some of the experiences that I have found most rewarding about life in the country. First of all, as I work at this book and find a sentence that won't fit together, I just lift my eyes the tiniest bit and look at a backdrop of giant maple trees. In the foreground is an old stone wall — a little bit shaky in places but just about the way it was put up years ago by those who came here as my predecessors to earn a living in the country. A view like this helps a lot to make country life worth the effort.

The sense of open space at the other side I appreciate, too. Here I can look out across my garden to a little pond where the ducks and geese seem to enjoy life in tranquillity. There's an orchard off to one side where the newly-ripened apples stand out red against the green foliage. Just to look at these trees at their time of autumn abundance or in the time of their spring blossoming seems to be quite enough reward in itself.

The winter season, which I enjoy most of all, has a glory all its own with the pure white blanket of crisp snow where I can ski or snowshoe to my heart's content just by stepping out the back door. When I get back from an excursion, there is the friendly warmth of a wood fire in the old cast-iron kitchen range. It's these and countless other intangibles that give country life its special savor.

And the intangibles seem to merge quietly into solid values too. For example, when I'm wandering through the autumn forest enjoying to the fullest the rich palette of Nature's color schemes, I am consciously noting down a wood supply for the future. Perhaps over here a deer trail could be used to get at a clump of trees that need to be thinned out, or down there a bridge thrown across the brook would be helpful in getting at some more of the wood lot, at the same time extending the network of winter ski touring trails. Then there's the garden which is a joy to see in its prime and also represents a rich menu of choice produce for the table, both summer and winter, at a very substantial savings in real dollars and cents, either in the best or the worst of times.

Good health is a very real asset and I believe that eating home-grown and home-prepared meats and vegetables is conducive to a more healthy body. The constant exercise that derives from getting up a woodpile, planting, tending and harvesting crops seems to have positive values in maintaining health and, although

I have no statistics to prove it, I am convinced that country life is the best for good health.

The economics of country life — making a living — in this book is related to the kinds of enterprises where people earn their money through productive self-employment either at their homes or farms or managed from their homes. These people are independent entrepreneurs of one kind or another. But at the same time I must note that many, perhaps most, of these little businesses rely to some extent on the regular salary brought in by a member of the family who has a job outside the enterprise.

This cash income is of great importance and particularly so at the beginning, when money is needed to get the ball rolling. Many of the little enterprises also are so marginal, in terms of income-producing ability, that someone needs to hold down a job elsewhere in order to make ends meet.

An example of this is my own work. At present I am a full-time writer. I cannot expect, though, that the royalty income from books and such other payments I get for writing ever would approach the $14,000 annual salary I had previously as a college librarian. On the other hand, my wife's salary as a school librarian brings in enough to keep us out of the poor house. But whether this combination of earning power will succeed in the long run is a moot point.

We live *in* the country, but our cash income does not derive from the land where we live. At the other end of the scale are the people — a farmer is the perfect example — who earn their living *from* the country.

Such a person is Charles Sanders (whose story is given in this book). He has been a dairy farmer and also has got much of his income from selling lumber, logs, firewood, and pulpwood. Yet another example is the market gardener who earns money from selling fruits and vegetables grown on his own land.

I'm continually amazed at the great variety of ways there are of making a living in the country. There seem to be countless options and I hope the catalog of the possibilities in this guide will give you some hope and encouragement to strike out on your own.

Temperament

There is a special temperament that characterizes the people who set out on an independent course in the country, something of the pioneer spirit in their blood. One or two hundred years ago, this type of person thought about new geographical frontiers and new homesteads on new land. And today the same restless, pioneer spirit seems to activate many of the people who are moving out of the cities to find a new life in the country.

The innovative person, which the new countryman often is, thinks of new ways to do old things better, at less cost in time and money. For him there are no sacred cows. He is the universal skeptic and the foe of stand-pat traditionalism.

As an example of an innovative person, I like to think of my ancestor, Luke Hale. He was a farmer seeking ways to ease the farm life routine. Of the several things he invented, there was an improved model of a washing machine for which I have the model and a patent signed by Andrew Jackson.

The venturesome person is the first one to jump into the pond in springtime just after the ice is out. He likes to try new things. He has a good dollop of the pioneer spirit in his make-up. He sees wish and fulfillment as a normal sequence.

Persistence is a country life necessity, too. But it needs to be tempered with a degree of flexibility that is cognizant of changing times and the needs of others.

Self-discipline is of utmost importance to the independent person. The majority of people rely heavily on structural incentives, and if they succeed, it is because some individual or institutional framework has prodded them into it or has provided an outline that needs only to be followed. If a man needs that sort of structure about him, I would doubt that country life could work for him.

Any society worth its salt needs to have a wide range of opportunities open to its citizens, and it's good to know that U.S. and Canadian life still has a place for innovative, venturesome, persistent and self-disciplined individuals whose numbers, I hope, are on the increase. Let me suggest now some other important needs. You could make an inventory of your skills, assets, desires and dreams.

Ideals

First of all, the dreams. Without a dream of what you want to be, where you want to be, the rest is fruitless. But it must be a possible dream. With a dream of country life with you night *and* day, you can bring the rest of the details into focus easily. Such a dream was the powerful incentive that drove me in search of Mill Hill or the Ultima Thule where the dream becomes reality. For the dreams of what you desire are the significant parts of your life. You must seek persistently to achieve them; otherwise your life is a nightmare.

But many a dreamer has foundered on the reefs of reality. And that's why the imperatives must be added that point the dreamer along a navigable course. You *must* be in touch with the circumstances of the times and know your own potentials. Can you fix things yourself or, if you cannot, can you find people to help you? You cannot pass the blame to the landlord. If the water pump doesn't work, you either fix it yourself or learn its intricacies from others.

There is no prescribed route, but it helps a lot if you know enough of the terminology of country life to be able to talk with a degree of sense to those who do know about it. What's the difference between a shallow and deep well jet pump? What's the difference between fuses and circuit breakers? Do you know what a sixteen-inch *run* of wood is, as opposed to a full *cord*?

The vocabulary of wood frame construction can be very handy, too, so that you can tell a sill from a plate and know that a stud can be a vertical support as well as a male animal used for breeding purposes.

If your background is urban and you dream to become rural, look into the vocabulary of country life. You can learn this best by listening and asking questions, with a good deal of emphasis on the former. If you are with some experienced countrymen, keep

your mouth shut for the most part and hear what they have to say. Be a learner and don't dwell on your own importance, or you may well find yourself an outcast in the place where you hoped to be accepted.

Money

These personal considerations are of prime importance, and to slight them would be foolish, but there are other important factors, too, such as money.

Most of the people reading this book are not well-to-do, and money probably has been a scarce commodity with them. I hardly need to point out that it has to be husbanded with care and spent with great prudence. Some who have helped in the preparation of this book advise to save up so that borrowing can be kept to a minimum, and this is good advice — within bounds. But if it will take a lifetime to save enough to achieve your dreams, something is wrong. You shouldn't have to drudge for years to do what you want only when you have reached senility. Yet many people do just this. It's a psychologist's puzzle to figure this out, and it's not my direct concern. For I'm interested in the sort of person who wants to DO IT NOW.

Choosing Occupations

First of all, a good deal of time spent with pencil and paper can save a lot of money and disappointment. At various times I have considered a number of projects, but careful analysis found them to be unreasonable.

At one time I wanted to organize a brick factory, for instance, because I found a deposit of good clay. But it turned out that the deposit was too small and the capital investment too high and the market surfeited with bricks.

I wanted to establish some charcoal kilns until I found that the regional demand for charcoal had been filled by large producers and I couldn't meet the competition.

I wanted to go into dairy farming, but my barn would have needed extensive alterations at great expense. I wasn't sure, either, that I wanted to spend seven days a week, three hundred and sixty-five days of the year, milking cows.

I wanted to start a ski import business until I found from my Senator what complicated red tape was involved in foreign exchange.

All of these and other projects are in my archives, and they are dead files because I analyzed the prospects quite thoroughly beforehand. I'm glad now I'm not a charcoal burner or a dairy farmer. Writing is quite satisfactory, and I never regret the time I spent learning library science. But still I doodle on paper about things I'd like to do at some time or another. It's a cheap pastime and rather harmless.

Where To Get Help

But if your pencil and paper analysis brings up a real winner, that's the time to get serious about the significant details such as *where* and how.

For the *where*, you should read two other books by Garden

Way: the first being, John Gourlie's HOW TO LOCATE IN THE COUNTRY, and the other, Herbert R. Moral's BUYING COUNTRY PROPERTY.

There are several things to add about the *where*. If you are going to open a country shop and sell a product at retail, you need to look into marketing prospects in the area. A roadside shop needs to be on a fairly busy thoroughfare and the people traveling down this road should be the type with a potential interest in your product.

I know of one very successful such roadside stand that has home-made wooden toys for sale. It's on a tourist route, and much of the business comes from people on their way home from vacations. The toy merchant has a large graveled parking lot on a straight stretch of the highway where people have a good chance to see his place. Another attraction is the beautiful view from his shop overlooking a pastoral river valley. This man makes most of his toys in the wintertime when tourist travel is almost nil. He gets up a good inventory so that he can spend his summers selling in his shop.

If you wish to depend on roadside sales, it will be a good idea to check long-range highway development projects with the planning engineers in the state highway department. They can give you crucial data on how much traffic certain routes generally carry and when. They also draw up projections for the future which may be of considerable help.

State, Federal, and local agencies can advise on a good place to locate your business. On the State level the development department, primarily concerned with aiding commercial projects, would be well equipped with statistical and other data. In Vermont, where I live, the state planning department is very active and I have utilized their services more than once.

There will be a department of labor and industry, a tax department, and finally there may be a department of environmental control whose rules and regulations will have a great deal of influence on where you can locate your business. Unfortunately, there seldom is one office that coordinates all of the state agencies and where you can go for one-stop aid and assistance, though the state library reference department comes the closest to a central information desk on various agencies.

On the Federal level the most useful agency may be the U.S. Small Business Administration with headquarters in Washington, D.C. This agency can help with advice about where to locate your business, as well as with a good deal more. You don't have to write to Washington, though, for the Administration has numerous field offices which are listed in local telephone directories. Senators and Congressmen can be very helpful, too. Don't overlook them. They often have state offices manned by staff members, in addition to their Washington locations.

Where to Locate

On the county level is the superb rural organization operated to help farmers and countrymen, the Agricultural Extension Service, each with a county agent, a home demonstration agent, and sometimes a county forester. The county agents work in close cooperation with the state agricultural colleges, and their combined expertise is astounding. Be sure to put them near the head of your list, not only for advice on where to locate but also, if your enterprise has an agricultural orientation, on how to get started and keep going. The Soil Conservation Service and the Agricultural Stabilization and Conservation Program usually are located near the County Agent's office. It's a complex bureaucracy, but worth investigating in detail since these agencies operate with your tax money for your benefit.

On the town or village level, you will find that local zoning ordinances probably will have a very significant influence on where you can locate what kind of business. The town clerk or manager is the person to see first, and he can refer you to others for further detailed service.

Private or semi-private organizations also should be on your checklist of sources of information about where to locate to assure a good market for your product. The Chamber of Commerce is an obvious place to start.

Some communities also have a group of businessmen organized for industrial development programs. While their aim usually is to get a fairly large business located in their community, they also could supply advice and aid on the smaller sort of enterprise that forms the subject of this book. The Rotary Club may be helpful also. An introduction from one Rotarian to another sometimes will turn up an amazing amount of worthwhile information about market prospects in a given community or region.

A local or regional market for some types of product projects may not be of immediate concern — for example a mail order business where the market can be anywhere the mails go. Here the important thing is to have items for sale that people want, wherever they read your catalog; things that people need either for work or leisure. This is a universal rule of business.

I have the opinion that one can get the most satisfaction out of making and/or selling things that are at the same time truly beautiful and functional. If you can make things that will become treasured family heirlooms, like my grandfather clock, you really have made a worthwhile contribution to human existence. True, some have got rich creating a specious need for shoddy, jerry-built stuff. But I have a feeling that the persons who read this book would never consider this as a way of making a living in the country. I hope not, anyway.

Factors for Success

Once a country-based enterprise is under way, there are certain general principles that favor continued success.

One must be alert to changing times and tastes. Fortunately the communications industry has been quite effective (almost too effective) in this respect. There is a veritable mountain of paper coming and going. Over and above this, there is the multiplicity of organizations that you can belong to, with their annual meetings and regional workshops.

It may seem a formidable obstacle, but one can pinpoint special interests by selective use of a few general bibliographies. In the book trade, for instance, the most important general bibliography is called BOOKS IN PRINT. There are several parts to this which include books currently available, listed by author, title, subject and publisher. For most people the subject list would be the most useful.

Since books are notoriously slow in getting written, published, and distributed, a speedier means of getting information is through periodicals and trade journals. The current index to these is ULRICH'S PERIODICALS DIRECTORY which is updated frequently. Next on the line we think of newspapers and here the AYER DIRECTORY has the answers.

For nearly instantaneous communication there are radio and television, both commercial and educational. The TV GUIDE and local listings in newspapers and special educational program guides provide the keys. I'll put in a special word for the Educational Television Network and the Canadian Broadcasting Corporation whose programs are far superior to the general run-of-the-mill broadcasts in the U.S. Unfortunately CBC broadcasts can be received by U.S. citizens only along the northern tier of states.

There is an organization for almost everything. It seems that when there is more than one person concerned with a subject, an association is duly founded. To find out where you belong, look in the DIRECTORY OF ASSOCIATIONS. And for some insight into the world of fabricated products, there is the THOMAS REGISTER OF MANUFACTURERS. All of these publications are expensive references but all of them could be consulted in a state or regional library or in a moderate-sized public or college library.

If you don't keep up to date, your business surely will suffer. But you might be ahead of the times, so think about the possibility of writing up something about your unique operation. Its publication, whether in a local newspaper or in a nationwide periodical, can do your business a world of good.

I've been rather concerned by the cultural isolation of Americans, and think it is eminently worth while to keep in touch with your colleagues around the world. Bob Keir (whose story is included in this book) told me how the Soviet fish culture technicians were far ahead of ours in matters of raising fresh-water fish for the table. Shouldn't all our farm ponds be producing so many pounds of edible fish each year? Let's find out how they do this. From another far distance read in Franklin H. King's FARMERS OF FORTY CENTURIES how Oriental culture has maintained a viable agriculture for thousands of years.

Economy

Here are a few thoughts about economy or making do: Wise use of the dollar bill entails some thought, but it doesn't take a college degree to know how much money you can save by growing all or part of your own food. If you read this book to the end, you can't fail to be impressed by our frequent arguments in favor of gardening. Learn how to make fuller use of wild plants and weeds, for what an array of edible food is available here only for the picking — with no effort at all in the growing! I hope you will take advantage of Euell Gibbons' landmark books, as I have. Among the countryman's wide range of options that are denied his city cousins is the growing of domesticated plants or foraging for wild ones. It is a marvelous substitute for those who have been dependent on supermarket quality and prices.

And in the realm of livestock production there is an equal range of opportunities open to the countryman. I find that hogs are the most economical source of meat, for they are omniverous feeders of surplus garden produce as well as kitchen scraps. And pigs can be brought to full size between May and November.

I have raised hogs for many years now, and can vouch for their utility. My only regret is when the time comes for slaughtering. Mutton and lamb are among other meats for the countryman's table, and where I live venison is an excellent meat source. These

deer are a serious nuisance, as they invade the garden without fear of human or canine intervention; so when I eat a venison roast in the autumn I also seem to taste the peas that I tried to raise in the summer. Have you tried woodchuck or raccoon, two other notable garden predators?

Another way to save money on the food bill is to join a cooperative where your and other volunteer labor helps to cut the cost of food distribution. Why pay the salary of a clerk in a supermarket when you can do the work yourself? I'd rather weigh out wheat flour and corn meal in a cooperative than wander down the aisles of a supermarket lulled by Muzak, taking my food pre-cut, pre-weighed, and pre-packaged.

Shelter is another place you can economize, especially if you build your own home. I wish that there were more of an incentive for people to build their own houses, as in Finland, where loans are readily available to those who wish to do so. Contractors in Finland primarily are concerned with public and commercial buildings.

If you cannot or will not learn the skills needed to build your own house, look for something that was built between World Wars I and II. Later the flimsy stuff took precedence, and I haven't seen many encouraging signs that home building will improve — unless you're willing to do it yourself.

The Land

Land — oh my! Here is the saddest tale of all. Everywhere one turns are stories of inflated land values, and nowhere are these prices going down. If you want acreage in the country now, consider yourself fortunate if you find even wild scrubland for less than three hundred dollars per acre. More often than not, this land will be remote, inaccessible, and practically worthless for any sort of agriculture.

I have seen prices in my neighborhood rise from forty dollars an acre to a thousand almost overnight. My own tax bill this year was *doubled* on a hundred-and-twenty-acre parcel. My wife and I bought this land in 1956 for $7,500, including the house in excellent condition. Now, in 1973, the house and land is appraised at fair market value at over $40,000. Who is benefiting from this inflation?

I cite these figures only to give you, the prospective purchaser of country land, some idea of the cash you will have to put up or the mortgage you will have to think of paying off to get a place in the country. I don't know of any way to economize on land purchase, but once you have it, you begin to acquire a certain equity value which later may serve as collateral to secure a loan.

Some have tried to save money on land purchase by joining with other families in the venture, but I have doubts on the long-term effectiveness of such a plan. More often than not, inter- and intra-family disputes get the parties mixed up in wrangles, ill feelings, and even law suits. In any land purchase, it seems best to keep the numbers of people involved to a minimum.

Some people have done well in buying a small piece of land on which to build their house, and then renting sections of adjacent land for specific purposes. This makes good sense, and sometimes you can make special rental agreements which will keep the actual cash cost of rental rather low, especially if you outline a special plan of land improvement. Such an agreement always should be in writing, perhaps using the standard rental forms that county agents have available. I rented some of my hay fields at one time, and the agreement worked out so that I had use of farm equipment such as tractors, plows, and harrows, for my own projects in exchange for the hay. Both parties were well satisfied with the arrangement.

Barter

This leads to the subject of bartering, which can be a very effective way to economize. Exchanging goods for goods, labor for goods, labor for labor, and all sorts of similar combinations used to be practiced very extensively and more than it is today. But there's no reason why it cannot be used as well now.

There is one classic story of the music teacher who bartered her instruction for dental work and other services. At one time I traded a used Jeep that I didn't need any more to a plumber in exchange for repair work to my bathroom.

Bartering has endless possibilities, and one of the main difficulties is getting the parties together in the first place. Often this can be overcome by using one of the popular country radio programs that specialize in trading. Usually there is no charge for a person to advertise what he wishes to trade. I have used such programs over the years with excellent results and I find that people respond quicker to an opportunity to trade than to buy. Charles M. Wilson's book, LET'S TRY BARTER; THE ANSWER TO INFLATION AND THE TAX COLLECTOR, is a very thorough treatment of the subject and it gives hundreds of different types of bartering possibilities.

Other Savings

There are literally hundreds of other ways to economize and *save* money, and I'll mention a few of these before turning you loose in the next part of the book, which contains stories and examples of the many sorts of things that people are doing to *earn* their living in the country. The two factors must go together.

For more than ten years we have purchased gasoline in bulk (three hundred gallon lots) from a wholesaler dealer. This represents a savings of several cents on the gallon over retail prices. The wholesaler provided the tank and hand pump without charge. All I had to do was dig the hole for the tank and fill it in after the tank and pump had been placed. This has been an extraordinary saving for us, though it may be less so now during the fuel shortage. If one uses fuel oil for heating, there can be a saving by installing a thousand gallon tank instead of the usual two-hundred and seventy-five gallon tank.

Many country folk have gone back to wood-burning kitchen ranges these days. Most of them can be fitted up with a water-heating unit in the firebox, and this in turn can be piped into a reservoir tank. The cost of heating water with oil or electricity is substantial, so if you can use wood for fuel, this is worth considering. If you prefer not to use the wood-burning range in the heat of summer, you might work out a combination oil-fired water heater to supplement the wood-burning unit. This is the best solution of all, for the recovery rate of a wood-fired unit is not as fast as by oil. The combination would give ample hot water at all times.

In these days of high power costs, it behooves you to think of ways to cut down on the use of electricity. For example, we seldom use the electric toaster any more because we know that any heating element takes a lot of power. Most of the time now we make toast on a piece of soapstone on top of the wood-burning range. We have an electric stove, too, but whenever possible we cook on the wood stove which also will bake bread and other things almost as well.

As a matter of fact, this wood stove probably is our most valuable appliance in terms of money saved over the years. In addition to being economical, it is esthetically attractive and a center of pleasant warmth in the cold winter. And what would the dog do without it? For him, happiness is under the stove.

As you read on, you will see how others have simplified the economics of life in the country and you probably will have your own pet ways to save. I'd be interested to hear what they are.

Part II

How People Do It

Success is an ambiguous term. Some may wonder why I haven't been more specific about whether such and such an enterprise reported on has been "successful." Well, I'll try to explain the way I see it, first of all, in dollars.

None of the people appearing in this book is wealthy. By dollar standards, I cannot say that any of the people included here are eminently successful. But the type of person who picks up this book, I believe, is not anxious to get rich — expects, rather, to find the intangible values of country life more important. On the other hand, none of the stories you will read about is a case history of bankruptcy, although some may be coming pretty close to it.

No, I have to interpret success on lines totally different from money values, and as you read the stories you will see what I mean. Success here is a satisfying life that is not overwhelmed by poverty. Some of the people whose stories are reported here may be very successful in making a living in the country, but at some point they might decide that what they were doing was not fulfilling, so they may abandon it for something else. All I can say now is that the stories you will read are real-life experiences reported as honestly as possible.

These stories are sorted into several broad categories, but you will see how parts of certain ones merge into other categories. Bob Keir, for example, is an environmental specialist, but his wife is a professional dressmaker. Orien Dunne started out in blacksmithing, but now he's more of an artist in iron. Charles Sanders primarily has made his living from products of the land but also has worked for wages. Is Maurice Page's shop more a business than a craft? Classification of these varied occupations in definitive terms in quite impossible, so I hope you will bear with my attempt to sort them out.

The stories are placed in these divisions: (1) Working for wages. (2) Services and business. (3) Professions, arts and crafts. (4) Products from the land.

Working for wages seems to be a universal element in all the stories, at some time or another. Some, like Elinor Belanus, find they can work for wages in a factory, yet live in the country at the same time. Industries are tending to move out of the metropolitan areas nowadays, and if they move far enough, their employees can have nice houses on an acre or so of land within reasonable commuting distance of their jobs. Mrs. Belanus's story points this out rather well.

Services and business makes up the greatest number of stories, and this is because service workers are in great demand. In fact, the best outlook for a small enterprise seems to be in the service area, though I had thought that products from the land would be the most significant. As you can see, it isn't and goes to the bottom of the list.

Professions, plus arts and crafts, rank very closely to services and business as a good way of making a living in the country. If you are a professional person, a serviceman (non-military type), artist, craftsman, or businessman, you have the most options for getting established in a country enterprise. This is not to say that market gardeners, pulpwood jobbers, basket makers and others who deal primarily in products from the land are obsolete. Far from it — it's just that the opportunities are more wide-ranging elsewhere. We'll see shifting alliances in our time, for change is inevitable. So if you are a versatile person, you will have more of a chance to succeed.

Take notes as you read these stories, for they contain much information. Just one of the notes might be about vacationing in the place where you intend to live later on — to see if you really like it. Mrs. Verna Hodges makes a good point here, and so does the Price family in California. When you get serious about a place, then visit it in the worst possible season to see if you still like it. If so, then it must be true love.

Working for Wages

Getting a paycheck at regular intervals gives a sort of security to life. True, the paycheck is never guaranteed to last forever, but it does serve a very useful function in making a living. Many people reading this book may not think that wage labor should be an important concern here. But, believe me, it *does* have a place in making a living in the country.

Regular work for wages can make all the difference at the initial stage of getting started in an independent business, or for getting it through a slack period, or for keeping a marginal enterprise afloat. Besides, factory work is becoming more available to country people nowadays. A 1970 report of the U.S. Department of Agriculture Economic Research Service said that manufacturing is growing at 3.1 per cent annually in non-metropolitan areas as opposed to a 1.3 per cent rate in the metropolitan areas. For the story of one person's experience here, read about factory work in the country and Elinor Belanus.

A Factory Job

Misfortune is something you have to contend with no matter where you live. The Belanus family experienced it when Mr. Belanus was killed in an accident not long after they had moved to upper New England from metropolitan New Jersey. Mrs. Belanus was left with the responsibility for her two girls, in addition to maintaining the home and working full-time in a precision instrument company where she did wiring, work similar to what she had done in New Jersey.

It was her husband's idea in the first place to move to the country, and she went along as a dutiful wife. Their younger daughter was delighted with the idea, as she loves the country. But the older daughter was unhappy about leaving her freshman classmates in high school. Now (in 1973) the older daughter has graduated from college and is married, while the younger one will start college in the fall. Mrs. Belanus thinks that her daughters stood a better chance in getting into good colleges with scholarship aid where they live now, than if they had stayed in New Jersey.

When the family moved in 1965 they sold their house with some difficulty and had only enough money for a down payment on a farm with house and two hundred acres of land. They had heard of the area through relatives who had a camp nearby.

Mrs. Belanus now has settled into a routine of life that leaves little time for outside activities. Aside from her regular job and the housework, she does some sewing and enjoys shopping trips to a nearby city. The major project, besides these things, is to raise quite a large garden every summer. Some years, she says, when she plants corn for the table, the garden is as large as an acre. Much of the harvest goes into the freezer for winter fare. As she points out, now, more than ever, the garden is a real money-saver because of the high prices of fresh, frozen, and canned vegetables.

Although Mrs. Belanus perhaps was a little dubious about moving to the country, she says now that her husband must have known what he was doing, for, despite the tragedy of his fatal accident, she is happier now than she would have been if they had stayed on in Megalopolis.

A particular point about this story is that, as certain industries have moved out of the cities, new employment opportunities with them make it possible to enjoy country life while earning a living from wage labor. For some people factory work in rural areas may provide an income during the initial period of establishing one's own business. With others, like Mrs. Belanus, the factory income makes it possible for her to maintain a rural home that is pleasant for herself and for her children who are always happy to come back to "the farm."

Working Toward the Move

The Dennis Gauthiers both were working for wages in 1972 in a wood manufacturing plant in Minnesota, while Mr. Gauthier was working his way into full-time farming by gradually increasing his livestock holdings.

When he wrote to Garden Way, they had ten sows and three

cows and plan to add more of the latter. They expect to continue working for wages until their place is paid for, and then they can be independent farmers.

Mr. Gauthier advocates buying used equipment for use around the place. He says it will do the same work as new and is a lot cheaper at that. If the Gauthiers are successful with their plan, they eventually will be earning all of their income from their forty acres of land and won't need to work for wages.

Richard E. Hart is a boiler fireman-engineer for a school in New Jersey. He gets a regular paycheck for this work, yet has the advantages in addition of being able to have a large garden and to enjoy the changing scenery of the seasons. He much prefers this way of earning a living to his former work as assistant manager of a variety store or as manager of a book store in metropolitan New Jersey. He is one of the many people who recommend highly to those who want to move to the country that they take the time to investigate the new locale thoroughly during vacations.

Mrs. Verna S. Hodges spent many years of her life working for state government for a regular paycheck. But while she was doing this, she also had many thoughts about where she really wanted to live. Now having reached retirement age, she is well provided for and particularly in terms of a place to live. Here's her story.

Planning the Future

While making a living in the country generally implies that some income-producing activity will be carried on, nevertheless it's worth considering what people do after retirement. In the past it was quite common for country folk to turn the farm over to the younger generation or to sell it and move to the village. Nowadays one is apt to see the reverse of the coin. Mrs. Verna S. Hodges spent thirty years working for the State of South Carolina. After retirement she left the city of Columbia and moved to the lakeside cottage which in the past she had used as a vacation place.

The story of how she acquired the cottage by the lake is unusual. Several years ago, when the South Carolina Public Service Authority developed a number of subdivisions around a man-made lake, Mrs. Hodges with her sister and brother-in-law obtained adjoining lots on a forty-year lease of seventy-five dollars a year. Some of the newer lots in the subdivision are renting for much more. Mrs. Hodges' lot is seventy-five feet by one hundred and fifty. The one next door is slightly larger. The brother-in-law built two cottages on a pay-as-you-go basis over a period of time on the adjoining lots, both fully insulated and with electrical service and plumbing.

Although many who lease the lots use them for recreation, a significant number of families live there year-round. Some of them have children who, Mrs. Hodges reports, greatly enjoy their life at the lakeside community since there are so many fine recreational opportunities like boating, fishing, water skiing, hiking in the woods nearby and along the nature trails not far away.

Mrs. Hodges figures that her retirement income is adequate for her rustic life at Lake Marion. She saves money by growing a garden and says that others there do likewise. The pace of life is easier than in the city, and she is fully satisfied with what she is doing with retirement years.

Those interested in finding out more about these subdivisions could write to or stop in at the South Carolina Public Service Authority in Moncks Corner, South Carolina.

That the Avon lady is calling may mean good news or bad news, but it's amazing how these energetic women get about the countryside with their wares. They supplement their incomes with these sales routes, and although their work is on commission, nevertheless it could be considered a form of working for wages. There are other sorts of country sales routes, too, such as Fuller Brushes, Knapp Shoes, and Rawleigh Products.

I'm inclined to think that these routes are not as profitable as they used to be, for the only peddlers I've seen for some time are the Jehovah's Witnesses, and formerly, missionaries from the Church of Jesus Christ of Latter-day Saints. Perhaps the decline is because country people are more mobile themselves today.

Another form of working for wages in the country is as a

harvester. Migrant labor excites the passions of many who claim,
with some justification, that this is a unique form of exploitation.
They make their point. But in some cases, as I can speak from
experience, itinerant (not migrant) labor helps to put a little
money in the pockets of people who can use it.

I have picked apples in the autumn for what I thought was a
decent wage but I would never recommend that one put his faith
in the migratory passage of the harvests as a way of earning rural
income. The main emphasis in this book is towards the person
who has some sort of roots. If it should turn out that there is a
chance to help with the harvest in your region and earn a little
money to boot, all to the good. But I wouldn't suggest following
the harvests from South to North as a means of a country
livelihood.

If working for wages is going to form part or all of the family
income in the country, seek out a location where you don't have to
commute long distances. Automobile maintenance and operating
expenses can take a big bite out of the pay check, not to mention

the time lost driving back and forth. Remember, too, that public transit tends to be scanty in country areas.

For a last and very interesting story in this part of the book, let's go to the West Coast and see how the Price family combines

Wage Earning and Homesteading

Patty Price tells an interesting story: how she and her husband and their four children left the San Francisco Bay area for a part of California where they "have no visible neighbors, no TV antenna horizon, no slum-gullion smog that smears summer into winter; only pines, rough and snowy peaked mountains, blue lakes, rushing pure streams where fish still swim, and our children can enjoy all these rare luxuries."

They now live in Shasta on two land parcels totaling nine acres which they bought in 1959 from the U.S. Bureau of Land Management for $2,100. Since moving onto the land they have developed a water supply system piped by gravity from natural springs; built a two-story home plus a large barn, a chicken run, and animal shed. Their house is all electric and complete with fireplace. For transportation they have a VW bus and, when road conditions are poor, a Land Rover gets them through. They also bought a twenty-year-old bulldozer to help with their projects.

The cost of these buildings, vehicles, and equipment added to the price of the land and a year's living expenses came to $13,000. They obtained this capital investment by selling their home and using savings.

This sounds, indeed, like getting their money's worth, and in order to stretch every dollar as far as it would go they practiced strict economy in their first year. Mrs. Price bought a treadle-type sewing machine at a rummage sale for five dollars and then taught herself to sew. She then proceeded to make all the garments her family needed, including her husband's shirts, the baby clothes, and even underwear.

They never took their washing to a laundromat. Instead, they built their fires early every Monday morning before the sun came up and heated water in antique cast-iron wash kettles that had been used in the city only for decorative purposes. They did the laundry in an old Maytag wringer-washer under the barn lean-to. Now they have more modern laundry facilities, but Mrs. Price nostalgically recalls the "clanging buckets full of fresh springwater and the crackling fires in the early morning dark."

Mr. Price, who has a high school and trade school education, worked as a journeyman refinisher in several factories in the San Francisco-San Carlos area for fifteen years before they moved to the country. Mrs. Price, with a high school education plus some college credits for night school, worked for eight years as a laboratory secretary in Palo Alto.

Undoubtedly Mr. Price's trade school training was most valuable in the numerous building projects they undertook. When he left his work in the city, he knew that any employment he might find probably would pay less than what he had been earning. Now he has work with the water department and earns about $8,800 annually — up from an initial $6,500. Their present income is sufficient for their needs, as they get good value from their large gardens and livestock.

Every year except 1972, when there was a water shortage, they have grown all sorts of things in their garden and additionally have foraged for wild fruits and berries. They freeze and can vegetables, make jam, preserves, wines, pickles, and chutneys. Livestock farming on a small scale produces meat, eggs, and milk from their pigs, chickens, ducks, squabs, and goats.

In order to cope with possible future water shortages, they have built a large storage tank and enlarged the supply system. Now they can irrigate when necessary and count on getting a harvest from their garden each year.

Mrs. Price offers this good advice for those contemplating a move to the country:

"Save — save — save. Sell everything that will bring a larger price in the city. Take trips (camping out) to the area you wish to move to and talk to the *local* people to find out the best ways of getting good buys on land. Talk to the Bureau of Land Management and find out if they are selling land where you want to settle. Often it can be had for back taxes. Try to sell your home for cash — even if you have to take a sacrifice in the amount. Plan to live in a trailer, garage, barn or improvised dwelling on your land, and build your own permanent home. It's so much less expensive if you can do this. If you don't garden, can, or sew, start learning how. These will be invaluable aids in saving money; making the whole idea possible."

Perhaps it would be well to add a note of caution after this story. The reader will see that the Price family bought their land in 1959. Their nine acres cost $2,100 then, but today land at such bargain prices is a rarity indeed, as noted elsewhere in the book. The Price family also is unusual in being able to make the dollar bill stretch so far. Their experience in this respect seldom can be duplicated even in the palmiest of times — and with today's inflation . . . ?

Services and Business

This area, of providing a useful service by way of a small business or by manufacturing some worth-while product, is where most country opportunities lie, now and for the future.

Renting

The James Lamberts in Illinois have settled into a systematic routine in the country. Mr. Lambert is a self-employed milk hauler, stopping at farms to pick up the milk and deliver it to a central collecting point.

The milk-hauling service is undergoing great change, since many farmers now hold their milk in refrigerated bulk tanks. Mr. Lambert's route is to farms that still ship in cans, and to keep up with the changing times, he will have to buy a more expensive bulk milk truck or be content with a dwindling number of customers.

But he has other ways of supplementing his income. He does general farm work, part for cash and part in exchange for rent on the place where they live in the country. They prefer this arrangement to trying to buy their own house and plot of land and they feel that this is a very economical way to provide for their shelter. They also get some of their food this way, by exchanging work for meat and other produce. The place they rent also has space for a garden about fifty feet square. The way the Lamberts found this situation was to comb the newspapers.

Sports Specialist

In New Hampshire a Dartmouth College graduate bought a farm which had excellent land for growing potatoes. For a number of years he made his income from this crop. But he had been one of the nation's top skiers, and he found that this skill and knowledge had a market. He began to do contract work as a consultant to ski areas on their trail system layouts. As this work grew and grew, he began to get more people involved with him, until now the consultant firm has a nation-wide reputation and many large contracts. He was alert to see that his skill could be parlayed into an excellent business.

Some other young people were interested in running a resort. They bought one that already had been successful as a purely summertime venture. In order to make it a year-round business, they added winter sports to their offerings. See how they are developing their business in the country as

Green Trails Resort

A resort catering to the tourist trade offers a way of making a living in the country that some people find very attractive. To illustrate some general principles of getting started in this type of business, I have chosen a nearby resort with which I am quite familiar.

Green Trails was established in the mid-nineteen-thirties as a small country resort for horseback riding enthusiasts and for students of botany. This particular combination of activities resulted from the fact that the proprietor and founder was a riding enthusiast herself and a professor of botany at a large university.

Miss Jessie Fisk converted part of her own home in Brookfield, Vermont, into rooms for her guests, and she remodeled an old pitchfork factory into a kitchen/dining room.

This enterprise was located in a tiny village with a large network of gravel roads suited for horseback riding and many acres of forest and field for botanizing. Her little project was very successful and her guests returned year after year to spend a week or so each summer. Miss Fisk kept her resort strictly as a summertime business and returned to teaching in the winter. Not long after her death, Green Trails was put up for sale.

At that time Chris and Sherrill Williams were in the market for something just like Green Trails. Chris was in the purchasing department of a large rural hotel. Before this he had worked with some of his relatives who owned several resorts in Vermont. He had enough experience so that he could evaluate the possibilities of developing the business into a year-round resort, utilizing the rolling hills and network of bridle paths and old roads for winter recreation in ski touring.

So in 1971 the Williamses bought Green Trails and began to plan for the future. The real estate consists of three old houses, a horse stable, the remodeled factory/restaurant, and the village general store which also includes the post office for the community. There are about seventy-five acres of pastures, fields, and woodlands included.

During their first six months at Green Trails, Chris and Sherrill managed the place themselves, hiring outside help to operate the stable and horseback riding activity. They also had a cook, kitchen help, and waitresses on the payroll in the summertime to operate the restaurant. Besides providing room and board for guests and meals for transient customers, they took on management of the store. This was quite a burden for them, especially when their plans for year-round operation called for the development of a winter sports program.

Chris and Sherrill invited friends to join them in the business, and early in 1972 Ed and Mary Ellen Taylor formally merged with the Williamses and the four of them organized as Green Trails Resort. They continued to manage and operate the store, but this was such a time-consuming sideline, they leased it to a man and his wife from town.

By late 1972 they had completed the major renovations of one of the houses and now can accommodate about thirty guests. They had to install a complete sewage disposal system to comply with strict environmental control laws. The installation and the major structural changes to the inn were done by contractors. However, the four of them have done the exterior painting and all the interior decoration of the inn.

The initial purchase of the land and buildings plus the contracting work and other significant expenses amounts to a quarter-of-a-million dollar investment, most of which has been obtained by bank loans. They have committed their savings to the project and have given themselves until 1977 as the initial trial period to see if they can meet current expenses and loan payments and begin to show a profit.

Some of their major problems involve the horseback riding program and the winter sports project. The former seems to be a declining attraction, and while ski touring certainly is a growing form of winter recreation, much depends on suitable weather and a good snow cover. Their first season left much to be desired in the form of ideal weather.

Another disadvantage is their off-the-beaten-track location not being immediately visible to the touring public. And yet their seclusion has some distinct advantages, for once people learn of the peace and quiet there, they come back again and again and spread the word among their friends.

Word of mouth has proven to be their most successful advertising. Of next importance is free publicity received from magazine and newspaper articles. Paid advertising has produced questionable results. They feel that they have to spend quite a lot on advertising; yet the results are difficult to assess.

They have tried to overcome some of the persistent problems by sponsoring various public activities to bring people to Green Trails. All of these events are in keeping with the atmosphere and environment of their little village and provide an attractive and restful setting for a clientele that appreciates such things.

Home Specialities

At first I thought that there weren't very many country barbers and beauticians until I began keeping watch for their places of business. Now I'm satisfied that there really is a good opportunity for those who have these skills to run very successful businesses right in their own homes.

Think of the money they must save by not having to pay for expensive town rentals. And the space in their own residences that is used for the shop can be considered a tax-deductible expense. True, anyone considering this rural service must be prepared to advertise in order to get a clientele started, and the shop should not be too far out in the country and it definitely should be on a good road. Adequate parking space must be provided, too.

Two types of home work that one sees advertised very frequently in the papers are addressing envelopes and servicing vending machines. Addressing envelopes is a service that can be conducted strictly in the home, while tending the machines requires a person to be on the road, although he could work from his country home. I've been a little skeptical of the amount of money that can be earned from these services and would strongly recommend that the person considering these jobs get all the details and some good references before taking them seriously. And it's doubtful that one could make a full income from this sort of business.

To turn now to another business that is very rewarding for the sort of person who has the skill, experience, and interest, read how Richard Alther moved from New York City to become a

Country Advertising Man

An advantage of city living is the opportunity to work at very exciting things and to receive good money for your efforts. In the late Sixties, Richard Alther was an account executive for the large advertising company of Young & Rubicam. He enjoyed the work he was doing for them, but had misgivings about how long it would take him to move up the executive ladder to even more rewarding work in a very competitive hierarchy.

To compound the Althers' uneasiness was "New York City crime, red eyes and a soot-filled apartment. We'd look across the Hudson River from our city window through the smear called air and literally gag."

With this compelling motivation it wasn't too difficult for them to pull up their New York roots (roots don't generally get very deep into the city pavements) and move to Vermont.

Vermont was their choice because Mr. Alther had visited almost every summer with his grandparents who had a summer house on the shores of Lake Champlain. Another advantage of that particular location was access to Burlington, the largest city in the state, and the likelihood of getting work similar to what he had been doing in New York.

Before they left the city, Alther wrote to advertising agencies, commercial television and newspaper people. After several uncertain, often trying, months, he was able to land a job with a Burlington agency, and this was the first step on the road to becoming completely independent. He supplemented his work with the agency by handling some accounts on his own, and within several years was able to incorporate his own business which consists of writing and placing advertisements for local Vermont firms, most often in the mail order business.

At the beginning he says, "It was an awful lot of traveling, letter-writing, phone-calling. However, I was able to offer these businesses a little more in the way of personal and prompt service than their Boston or New York-based agencies." His efforts to get established were successful not only because of his diligence, but also because of a rapidly growing rate of local business activity and the proximity of the area to the major metropolitan areas of the Northeast, which boosted his resort, retail and mail order clients' sales.

Alther mentions two particular satisfactions as a result of his move to the country. The first is the opportunity it has afforded to manage his own business rather than having to cope with many levels of management in New York. Another satisfaction is income level which is more than adequate to enable them to live well. Then, of course, there are the many other rewards of country life which they find so appealing.

One of the Althers' particular pleasures is their garden which they call a hobby but which, at about half an acre, gives them an ample surplus for winter food requirements. Now they also have thirty fruit trees, chickens, a grape arbor and bees, but no livestock.

When they first moved to the country place they made the mistake, common to many, of planning too big and not having the proper time to care for all they had planted. "The weeds won out." Now they have got things in balance and only have to tend the garden on weekends.

It cost the Althers four to five thousand dollars to get settled in Vermont, the money used as a down payment on a very old farmhouse and four acres of land. With the salary-commission from his first job, the Althers spent additional money getting materials to salvage and remodel the farmhouse.

Mrs. Alther was prepared to work if necessary in the early years of getting established in the country, but as it turned out didn't have to. She worked on an area theater project and has done a number of free-lance writing projects for local publishers.

Although the particular work that Alther does is rewarding both financially and personally, he notes that this very type of work is rapidly eroding the essentially rural character of Vermont, which is what has made it so attractive to so many people in recent years.

The Althers offer some good advice to those contemplating a move to the country: In the first place, don't think of yourself as a specialist, but cultivate a wide range of abilities so that if one of your attempts at earning a living fails, you can fall back on other competencies. Not only cultivate the ability to move gracefully from one occupation to another, but also learn the necessary skills so that you can manage such a wide range of the important chores connected with your principal business that you don't have to hire outside help. A person who carries the job through all the way from beginning to end often can deliver a better product, whether it be advertising copy or a butternut squash.

Another suggestion the Althers make is to look into the possibilities of moonlighting in a field comparatively close to what you already do. Alther notes an architect of his acquaintance who sells color photography to calendar-makers and magazines.

A consistent remark that Alther, along with many other country dwellers, makes: "Simplify your way of life and dramatically cut your income requirements (rather than feel you are sacrificing income to move to the country). Snowshoeing is quite a bit cheaper than downhill skiing or snowmobiling, and so on."

A final caution, and a very pertinent one, is to limit the number of guests that you entertain from the city. When a family has moved to the country and has built up a scene of pastoral delight, one of the minor — and sometimes major — inconveniences of their new life is the way relatives, friends, and sometimes even casual acquaintances find it easy to drop in and stay a while.

"Your country place can easily become a habit with them," Alther warns. "Put them to work in the garden; send them out skiing, but don't feel you have to join them at twelve dollars a day for three runs."

Every countryman has to deal with the problem of visitors in a hospitable yet firm manner. Summertime is an especially hectic season. Then the heat and smog of the city is intense, and the green fields, cool forests and rippling streams are most inviting. The problem's solution always requires tact and diplomacy, for how can you send little Elroy (who has hay fever) out to rake up the scatterings, or Aunt Hattie (who has varicose veins) into the garden to pull weeds?

No doubt about it, country living has its trials, but I'm sure that the Althers would much rather deal with country-based problems than with Megalopolis, canopied with "the smear called air."

Mixed Jobs

Edith and Howard Bloom moved from Metropolis many years ago to an attractive little house at the end of a country road. Edith got work as the secretary to the president of a small college, and Howard earned money typing papers for the college students, making a success of this service because of impeccable and rapid typing skill. From time to time he also helped faculty members with their research projects by getting the final drafts ready for publication.

More recently Edith has retired, Howard has secured a job with the State tax office, while Edith now has taken over to some extent the service of typing papers for students and faculty.

Obviously, this little business could thrive only where there is a college, university, or research center, for the typist needs to be in close touch with clients.

Photography and the other graphic arts is a very competitive field, but Arnold and Priscilla Spahn think they can make their business succeed in the country as well as elsewhere. Look at the way they are trying to make a go of it as

Free Lance Photographers

At first glance it would seem that free lance commercial and industrial photographers would be successful only if they were located in a large urban area next to their clients. Arnold and Priscilla Spahn don't believe that this is true and have gambled that they can make a success of this business in a very rural part of upper New England.

There isn't a factory or a smokestack anywhere near their home and studio which is situated on a good gravel road, surrounded with beautiful fields and woods. Travel by auto is the way they visit their clients and they will go as far as Boston in search of work to supplement what they can generate closer to home.

Before they moved to their present home, the Spahns made inquiries of other photographers and checked the yellow pages of the phone books to find whether or not there would be room for them to fit their enterprise into the existing pattern. This analysis satisfied them that there would be enough work to keep them busy.

They bought their remodeled farmhouse home in August of 1972 and since the house already was in good condition, they could move right in without having to make extensive alterations. The next major project, a studio of their own planning, was begun in November, with the major structural work being done by a contractor. They did much of the finish work themselves and had the place ready for business by the next June. They estimate that this first major investment in house, land, and studio is divided into sixty-five per cent in the house and land, with thirty-five per cent in the studio. The money for this new project came from savings and from the sale of their former home and a valuable piece of property along the Connecticut River. The funds were enough so that they did not have to borrow initially.

They have planned on three years, beginning mid-1973, as the starter period to get their business established and they estimate they will have to gross $25,000 a year to be successful. They are optimistic about the prospects, and when I saw them last they were busy on their first assignment.

Both Arnold and Priscilla have been serious photographers ever since they were youngsters — they are now in their mid-thirties — but this is their first venture at making a living from photography. In order to prepare, they spent a year studying at a professional photography school, which they look on as a sort of finishing school experience to hone their skills. Their school living expenses were paid for under Arnold's G.I. Bill benefits, based on his time with the U.S. Air Force.

Priscilla has a college background in art and elementary education, while Arnold has a high school equivalency degree, some college credits, and experience in electronics from his Air Force service. Much of their technical skill and expertise in photography has been derived from self-instruction.

Arnold estimates that seventy-five per cent of his specialized training in photography came from skills he taught himself. Priscilla figures she is about sixty per cent self-taught. Their large library is ample evidence of a continuing interest in keeping up-to-date — not only in new photographic developments but in a wide range of subject fields. Attending photographers' conventions, reading trade journals and technical reports from photographic supply houses, all keep them current with recent changes and developments in this high competitive field of work.

Photography is the Spahns' only enterprise. They don't supplement their income with other work, and they divide the responsibilities of the actual photography and processing equally. About half the assignments are done on site, the rest in the studio. Arnold spends more time on sales trips than Priscilla does, but, on the other hand, she handles the bookkeeping and spends more time on housework, although Arnold takes on about a quarter of the household chores. They appear satisfied with their division of effort and refer to their work as fun — an ideal to which many people aspire but few achieve.

Apart from their profession, the Spahns find that simply living in the country is a great solace after being urbanites. Their eleven-year-old daughter, Katie, likes country life too, and enjoys the small school she attends in contrast to the large city school where she began her education.

Arnold and Priscilla still maintain an interest in sports car racing, although they find that the opportunities for hunting and fishing, now close at hand, take up most of their leisure time. They plan to work on a joint project with neighbors to build a skating rink on a nearby pond. None of them seems to miss the particular recreational opportunities offered by city life, although their ties with the city are somewhat stronger than with their country neighbors because of their business connections.

The Spahns' ten-acre piece of land surrounding the house and studio gives them plenty of space for a large garden, and their first year's harvest is giving them a good surplus for freezing and canning, in addition to the fresh produce for the table. In the six of their ten acres that are in woodland they have begun a forestry-improvement project by thinning, pruning, and relocating some trees. They have learned to identify a number of the edible mushrooms and in season go on foraging expeditions for these and also for wild berries.

From a philosophical point of view, the Spahns see the return to the countryside, on a national scale, as perhaps contributing to an improvement in moral character. They agree with others that it's unlikely and would be impractical for a mass migration to take place from the cities to the rural areas. But for a significant number of disaffected urbanites, making a living in the country offers a reasonable solution for so many people like themselves.

Staying Rural

Sadly enough, many young people are forced to leave the rural parts of the country where they grew up in order to find work. At one time there seemed to be a wholesale migration or flight to the city.

Now I detect a considerable reversal of this phenomenon which, in fact, is the subject of this book. While many people are moving from the city to the country and are seeking ways to make their living out here, there are others who always have lived in the country and have found ways to stay there and make a decent income.

Elliott Morse runs a small car repair service in his own shop located across the country road from his house at the outer fringe of a small city. He was brought up as a member of a farm family and wanted to stay near the homestead. His solution to staying put seems an excellent one, since auto mechanics are in great demand. Morse's business is so rushing that one has to wait almost a month before getting an appointment with him. But so many like his work and his friendly manner that they are willing to wait for it whenever they can.

Another family that has spent most of its life in the country and has found a way to stay there are the Wiggetts. These fine people

Keep Folks Warm

Wiggett Brothers is a well-known name in their central New England area. Douglas and Gordon Wiggett have been installing home heating systems for more than twenty years and anyone familiar with the region's winters knows a good heating system is an absolute necessity.

For the Wiggetts, the heating business has turned out to be an ideal way of making a living in the country. They can organize their work around their pleasure. Somewhat predictably, the furnace installations drop off at the time of deer hunting in November and again when salmon fishing is at its prime in Canada's Maritime provinces.

Douglas and Doris Wiggett live in a small hamlet, and Gordon and Grace live twenty miles down the road in another village. The fact that they live that far apart doesn't seem to be much of an inconvenience to their business. The red phone hot line keeps them in touch as much as they need to be outside of working hours, to organize jobs and prepare schedules.

Before they got the heating business established, both Gordon and Douglas did all sorts of things to earn a living. Douglas sold Singer sewing machines door to door in the Boston area. For two years they both worked in a Connecticut machine tool industry. Then each went his own way for a while, Gordon training himself to be an expert linoleum-installer, while Douglas joined forces with another man as logging and pulpwood jobbers. After this stint, which lasted about five years, Douglas and Gordon commuted to work in the machine tool industry in Springfield, Vermont.

Douglas got tired of the odd shifts and the long commuting distance and decided he wanted to work at selling again and be closer to home. So he boldly walked into an appliance dealer's store and said he was ready to begin selling on commission. The dealer put him to work.

Selling appliances seemed to open the way to installing heating systems, but first Douglas had to persuade his brother to join forces with him. Once that had been accomplished, the next step was to line up a job, get a furnace on credit, and do the work in such a manner that the customer would be completely satisfied.

Payment for that first job provided capital to start the next one and to pay off the debt. As their business grew and as they have needed money from time to time for expanding their operation, they have secured bank loans and also some help from the U.S. Small Business Administration.

In the early stages of their business they took on plumbing as a sideline. But they gave this up when they found they were getting too many people on the payroll — and because bill-collecting for small plumbing jobs was next to impossible. They have very few debts in the heating business because in most cases the purchaser has to borrow money directly for that purpose, and payment for Wiggett Brothers is assured.

The Wiggetts have found that word-of-mouth is the best advertising. It's free and very effective and becomes more so the longer they are in business. The only other advertising they have done consistently is to sponsor a half-hour radio program once a week. Much of their work is done on farms, and this radio program is admirably suited for the purpose because it's a kind where people can trade and sell things.

Between this radio program and word-of-mouth, the Wiggetts have all the work they care to do in a fifty mile radius of their homes.

Both Douglas and Gordon have high school educations plus some night school courses in the liberal arts, which they took in Connecticut when they were trying their hands in industry. Factory work didn't appeal to them very much, but they count their experience in machine tool work of some value in their present business.

Doris and Grace Wiggett help with the income. Grace keeps the books and does all the accounting for Wiggett Brothers. She also is a licensed real estate broker and has her own sideline selling property in surrounding towns. It is a good business, and she enjoys it very much.

Doris is a registered nurse with a degree from the University of Maine. Her B.A. in education plus the nursing background has prepared her for her present work as instructor in practical nursing at the area's hospital.

Both branches of the Wiggett clan have raised large families, most of them now grown up, married and established in their own lines of work.

Now in their fifties, the elder Wiggetts have no special plans for retirement, though Douglas has an idea that he might give up the installation part of the heating business and devote his time to designing and selling systems for others to install.

One of the principal satisfactions that come with the lives the

Wiggetts lead has been their large circle of friends and acquaintances. As someone remarked: "Going to the Wiggetts' is like going to Cairo. Sooner or later you meet everyone in the world." For a number of years the Douglas Wiggetts' house was a library outpost with the bookmobile stopping there every couple of weeks to exchange books. Neighbors would stop to get new reading material, have a cup of coffee, and chat a bit.

Not all of their friendships were made in the line of business, either. Doris and Douglas took a fancy to square and round dancing some years ago and have made many new friends in that way. They even converted part of the barn behind their house into a small dance hall and regularly hold dances there.

Another of their sidelines has been the breeding and raising of Golden Retrievers. They have about twenty dogs in their kennel now, and have raised and sold or given away almost a hundred. The land which used to be their garden now is their kennel. But on an adjoining plot they have a joint gardening project with neighbors. The Wiggetts provide the land and the neighbors raise strawberries, to the mutual satisfaction of both parties. The Wiggetts take their payment in kind.

The male Wiggetts are indefatigable outdoorsmen. There's hardly a stream or pond in the north country that hasn't felt their fly lines laid gently on the surface, and they know well all the game covers from Lost Nation to the Yellow Bogs. When the hunting season has closed there is an opportunity to go ski touring, and "Iron Man" Wiggett gets around easily on the slim cross-country skis despite a serious fracture incurred some years ago while downhill skiing.

The Wiggetts have designed a way of life where work and pleasure mingle in a balanced proportion, giving them enough income to enjoy doing the things they like best.

Some of these country businesses have gone through more than one generation: father has taught son and the son has carried on the business, although the skills and products of these older businesses usually are altered from time to time to keep pace with changing markets. Maurice Page is the subject of

From Butter Boxes to Eggs

Mr. Page is the second generation of a woodworking family in a small mountain village. He divides his daylight hours in the summertime between a woodworking business, where his principal production is cooperage (mainly watering tubs for livestock), and raising poultry for hatching eggs. His income derives about equally from both activities, and he is also receiving some Social Security payments.

The sign over the door of his place of business reads, "Page's Box Shop," but this is a relic of former times when he and his father made a considerable number of cheese and butter boxes and also wooden cattle stanchions.

This business has declined — in his neighborhood, at least — and now he finds the best market is for his carefully built watering tubs, most of which are six feet in diameter and two feet in depth, being slightly larger at the top than at the bottom. Most of the lumber for the tubs is white pine which grows well nearby, but sometimes he uses hemlock, another fairly common tree in the region. He buys the rough lumber from sawmills and forms these boards and planks into finished staves in his own shop, using such tools as band saws, planers, jointers and shapers.

The machinery is powered by electricity nowadays, although in former times they used water power (the dam washed out in a flood) and steam power. Mr. Page still has the water turbine and the steam engine which he plans to sell if he can find a buyer. He thinks it would be impractical and too expensive to rebuild the dam or to re-install the steam system.

Another man in this area runs a combination sawmill and box shop and still uses water power to run the whole works. When the water is too low to turn the wheel, he switches over to a diesel engine. Yet another mill operator (this shop builds harpsichords) is planning to install water power.

Mr. Page's workshop suits him all right even though it may be considered old-fashioned. When the shop was converted to electricity, an electric motor was hitched onto the old power transmission system which is the same today as it was years ago and consists of pulleys, shafts and belts. When the shop is in operation, everything seems to be moving. But according to modern safety standards all these belts, shafts and pulleys should be enclosed.

When I was visiting the shop, I made a point of looking at Mr. Page's hands, for workmen in the woodworking trades often have one or more thumbs and fingers missing. Mr. Page has all of his, which must mean that a careful workman can work in safety even when the hazards are high.

Nevertheless, under the Occupational Safety and Health Act of 1970, Mr. Page cannot employ persons to work in his shop at the machinery, though he does hire a man to help him put the tubs together in a shed at one side of the shop. But he can't expand unless he completely remodels his shop to comply with the new standards — of which he is quite critical, thinking of them as bureaucratic interference. If all workmen were as careful as he is, there would be no need of regulations, but experience has proven otherwise and the regulations are here to stay.

If anyone plans to open a shop and employ people, then, it will be necessary to comply with all of these regulations which are complex indeed. Essential points in the law (Public Law 91-596, 91st Congress, S. 2193) are summarized in a booklet entitled *Recordkeeping requirements under the Williams-Steiger Occupational Safety and Health Act of 1970*. It is published by the Occupational Safety and Health Administration and is available from the U.S. Department of Labor in Washington, D.C., or from Congressmen and Senators. Administrative changes in the law are published from time to time in the *Federal Register*.

Any new enterprise must comply with these regulations or face prosecution and heavy fines. Older businesses sometimes are allowed variances which may give them time to comply.

Mr. Page intends to continue his business by himself. The market for his watering tubs is good, while there is an increasing demand for novelty items. He fabricates a number of different-sized boxes with hinged lids, some of which are used for sewing boxes. These he sells to another who has a retail outlet in a large resort town. He also cuts out stock for footstools and cribbage boards which others finish. He feels he really should be selling directly to the customer in order to achieve the best profit from his work, and he intends to experiment with this in the future as a sideline to the watering tubs.

Another aspect of his way of making a living is the poultry business. There is a slightly different twist on the usual egg production line in that Mr. Page is concerned with hatching eggs. He is under contract to a large hatchery to produce fertile eggs, and therefore he must keep roosters with the hens. The eggs are shipped to the hatchery for artificial incubation. This enterprise is a year-round business for him, while he has to quit work in the shop when the cold weather sets in. There is no way to keep it warm since the steam engine was replaced by electricity.

This combination of poultry and woodworking, although it may seem an odd mixture, has provided Mr. Page with a decent income and work that he enjoys. He's happy with it.

A small business that has interested me a lot is snowshoe manufacture. Right now the few companies existing in the United States and Canada are hard-pressed to keep up with orders, since more and more people are finding out what fun it is to walk on the snow.

Making Snowshoes

Floyd Westover in New York state has made a success of his snowshoe business through a significant and functional change in design. Walter York in Maine retired from the lumbering business and makes a few snowshoes along traditional lines each year in his shop. Baird Morgan in Vermont bought an existing snowshoe company and has concentrated on sales, while diversifying the business with a line of fiberglass canoes. In the Province of Quebec the center of snowshoe manufacture is in the tiny Huron village just outside Quebec City. Here members of the Indian tribe work in several establishments, making the frames and lacing up the snowshoes in a very profitable business. Other Indians in the Yukon Territory have been overwhelmed with orders for their special brand of snowshoes and have had to turn down most of them.

Making snowshoes would be an excellent country business for a small family that liked to work in wood and leather. Such a small enterprise could succeed not by direct competition with the larger snowshoe companies but in the design of new styles, as Floyd Westover did, and in making the snowshoes of superb hand-crafted quality. A possible sideline to the business would be a snowshoe museum that would cater to the tourist trade and demonstrate the intricate ways that snowshoes are laced in traditional patterns. Direct sales to customers also would be a way of increasing profits.

Running a museum as a private enterprise has other possibilities too. For instance, there is the Crafts Museum in Mequon, Wisconsin, which advertises as "A living, *travelling*, museum of early American tools used to work wood, ice and leather. Educational, entertaining museum programs for schools, conventions, meetings, fairs, shows, etc."

The museum offers displays, slide lectures and/or motion pictures and live demonstrations. With the increasing interest both in the United States and Canada in our heritage of craftsmanship, it would seem that a combination of a museum and a small craft business would have excellent possibilities wherever there is sufficient tourist traffic. Or, as in the Wisconsin case, the museum could go to the public.

The combination of a small business with an educational sideline sometimes is an effective way of making a living in the country, as in the case of basket making, a traditional craft today all but eliminated as a regular business since there are very few of the old craftsmen left. The main qualification for such a business would be that the proprietor should be a thorough scholar of the subject in addition to being a superb craftsman, and be willing to spend time teaching the subject to apprentices. But there is more about apprenticing in the next section.

Before we close this one, however, read the intriguing tale of the way David Bredemeier used his skill in design as a

Jack-of-all-Trades

David Bredemeier of Charlotte, Vermont, has been self-employed for about four years now seeing if he can make a living from what he enjoys doing. In his case the pleasant work is building architectural models, designing and building lamps and toys, doing contract woodworking and cabinet making, photography and writing. One of the more unusual things he has made is a nineteen-foot-long fiberglass "iceberg" for a New York City health spa. The variety of things he does suits him well.

Mr. Bredemeier had been in Vermont earlier visiting a potter friend, and he was pleased with his introduction to this area near Lake Champlain. He looked for work, could find none, and returned to his parents' home in Buffalo, New York.

Back in Buffalo he did some thinking and decided that ". . . if one can't obtain exactly the job he wants, one might do worse than take the best job available in an area he really likes." Following his own advice, he borrowed a hundred dollars from relatives, loaded up his old car, and headed back for Vermont in earnest. It took him a couple of weeks to land work with a large architectural firm, drafting, model-making, and photographing. He continued at this for four and a half years, while starting his own business during off-hours from the architect's office.

Bredemeier summarizes it by saying that he "started with a hundred dollars, a car, friends and the Desire." I would stress desire as the primary and most important ingredient. Without it the others are largely ineffective — like a dinner without potatoes.

Bredemeier's educational background has particular relevance to his present work. After primary and secondary education in a progressive country day school in Buffalo, he graduated from Antioch, a college where the students take jobs between academic semesters. Then he worked for an architectural model-maker, two architects and a county planning organization. For a year he studied at the University of Edinburgh in Scotland.

When he started working in Vermont, Bredemeier rented rooms or sections of houses. After a year he was able to buy for slightly under $15,000 a small house and a two-story, three-car garage, which included two and a half acres of land. He helped to pay for the purchase by renting the house while he converted the space over the garage into a studio-apartment for himself. The house and land since has doubled in value because of his improvements and the general upward trend of real estate prices.

Bredemeier recently has married a Vermont girl whose profession is audiology and therapy for children with hearing impairments. Lydia Earle Bredemeier works nearby in Burlington (Vermont's nearest approach to urban — an area population of 99,000) at a medical center hospital. Her particular skill is in great demand nowadays, and she has no lack of opportunity for employment.

They both enjoy living in a rural area, though they appreciate the proximity to the cultural aspects of the city and particularly those of the state university. They also enjoy the availability of sailing, walking, reading, skating, skiing, gardening (initially in 1973), photography, and "watching the mountains go by across the lake."

By way of advice for prospective country folk, Bredemeier says, "If you don't have a job lined up, it's helpful to have friends or relatives nearby. Be prepared to take work more generalized in nature than your previous training or job. Better still, if possible, keep serving metropolitan needs while living in the country.

While not every occupation is susceptible to this treatment, it's surprising how many people are doing just that."

Professions, Arts and Crafts

Professional work generally implies a good deal of academic training — certainly an undergraduate degree and usually graduate work at least to the Master's level. Exceptional people sometimes achieve professional status by rigorous home study and a great deal of specialized work experience.

Normally we think of the professions as being more at home in the city than in the country, but this is not necessarily the case. There is a New England dentist who practices his profession in a very rural town which isn't even listed on the map. The dentist, his wife and young son wanted very much to get out of the city and back to nature. They achieved their wish and now are living in a mountainside cabin heated with a wood stove and with no running water or electricity.

At first the dentist didn't intend to practice, but when his neighbors found out about his profession, they persuaded him to set up an office and he obliged.

In the whole array of specialists who assist in preserving health and abating sickness, special mention should be given the traveling nurses who go from house to house in rural areas to help bedridden patients and other convalescents who do not need hospital or nursing home care. These district nurses, as they are sometimes called, are a great boon to country folk, and for the trained person who likes to get around on the back roads, this type of nursing could be just the thing to earn a living in the country.

I have little data on the rural ministry. Circuit riders who used to bring faith and comfort to country dwellers seem to be a thing of the past, although Jehovah's Witnesses and the Mormons make the greatest effort to be in touch with the country.

Generally speaking, there is a surplus of teachers and it's pretty difficult to get a job in the public school system, whether urban or rural. In the past and to some extent today, however, the rural teaching jobs come easiest, probably because many teachers prefer to work in larger school systems and the pay is better. The best opportunities seem to be in special teaching with remedial work, and even the rural school districts now are hiring people who have special qualifications.

Teachers who want to combine rural life with their profession perhaps should think seriously about private school work. There are many of the so-called "alternative" schools in the country today. Most of them are founded on idealism and most founder for lack of financial support; yet these small, private schools come close to the kind of country enterprise that I have been writing about. It's worth considering them with some care. Here is a personal example:

Teaching

Some twelve years ago we cooperated with a near neighbor to establish an elementary school as an alternative to our town's public schools, for we had serious reservations about the quality of teaching and the curriculum.

Our neighbors were the prime movers in this project and one undertook to do most of the teaching and conducted classes in her home, while my wife relieved her of some household responsibilities. In addition to our own children, there were a very few other students. At the time, there were few state regulations to comply with, and all of these had to do with the physical facility.

The school was short-lived, like so many others of this type, for when the public school facilities were improved we saw no need of continuing our own and we knew that our children needed the extended social contacts that they would get in the public schools.

For the limited time that the school ran, it was an educational success, but it couldn't qualify as a real way of earning a living in the country. For such an alternative school to succeed, it must have enough parents who feel the need of such a school badly enough to support it with their time and money. Working in this sort of school can be a very exciting experience for a young teacher, but probably it's not a very good way to make a living.

Another profession with a singular affinity to the country is writing. The initial investment is low — all you really need is a typewriter and paper and a place in your own home to work. Some types of writing require a good deal of research, however, and in this case it is helpful to be near a fairly large library, though one often can rely on getting books by mail from a state or regional library.

Getting a first book or article published is the important initial step. Once a writer gets established in this way, succeeding contracts and assignments come easier. But, as noted earlier, the potential income from writing is quite minimal, unless one produces that rarity, a best-seller, and then also derives income from screen and TV rights.

A writing colleague who lives with his family in Maine seems to have evolved a life style quite in keeping with his environment. Let me introduce the story of

Living and Writing

While many who have offered opinions on how to make a living in the country stress the importance of hard work, Theodore Enslin of Temple, Maine, indicts the work ethic and accuses it of being a destructive force when misapplied. He feels it *has* been and *is* in the United States and other countries. In his view it is ridiculous to work long hours to earn money to get commodities that are not really necessary. Much that is taken for granted as being indispensable for the "good life", he feels, is a foolish waste of time.

The first important step to living a rational life in the country is to discard the frills of modern civilization. By doing this, a yearly cash income of two thousand dollars or less, he estimates, should be ample for a family of three or four — despite inflation.

Enslin lives with his wife and young sons about a hundred miles from the Maine seacoast. He made a number of land purchases there from 1951 through 1966 and eventually acquired two farms with a total area of nearly a thousand acres. For these he paid $4,000, which is not possible today, of course.

They make this philosophy of simplicity work for them by eschewing practically all modern utilities except for electric lights and a telephone in the farmhouse where they generally live. They don't use power tools, nor do they have indoor plumbing or oil heat. When they feel the need for an article of furniture or household implement, they make it themselves with hand tools. They gather much of their food supply from wild sources and suggest that fully three-quarters of all the vegetable needs of the average family could be gleaned from pastures and woodlands.

Enslin is the gardener of the family and he notes that this activity is extremely important to them. The garden, forty feet square, is never plowed. Each fall a foot of compost and manure is spread, and in the spring the seeds are planted through this cover. Enslin makes the distance between rows about half of the usual recommendation.

Of gardening he says, "My contention is that people plant entirely too much, for which they usually have no use. A good rule of thumb: if you're tempted to plant twenty rows of beans, plant two and take care of them." He adds that he never spends more than an hour a day tending garden.

Although their farms are a hundred miles from the seacoast, the Enslins willingly go that distance several times a month to gather shellfish to supplement their diet of tame vegetables and wild plants. Of the latter, they follow the general pattern of foraging laid down by Euell Gibbons.

Animals for food or as pets have no place in their life style as they believe that the time and effort required to care for them offsets any possible advantages. They have a source of lamb from a farm about twenty miles away, and in mid-1973 were paying about thirty-five cents a pound for this meat (dressed weight).

It is impressive to note that the Enslins believe an outlay of less than one hundred and fifty dollars a year sufficient to purchase the staple foods which supplement garden produce and wild sources — and this for a family of four! Their cost of living index must cause the statisticians to blink.

Enslin did not follow the standard educational sequence, but the classical English system, and after this opted out of formal higher education to study composition with Nadia Boulanger. He has studied the classical and several modern languages, has done a stint as a musician/composer, and presently is earning his living as a writer. He is the author of twenty-one books.

Enslin gets some income from readings and lectures at colleges and universities and this has increased in recent years, involving a great deal of travel several times a year. His income, derived solely from literary activities, is adequate for their needs and also provides enough to buy books — many of them expensive — and to enjoy a fine music system. He doesn't do any outside money work, other than that mentioned above, but there are always projects such as helping a neighbor rebuild his burned house. Such voluntary efforts not for pay are quite common for country people who feel impelled to help each other out after a disaster.

Enslin didn't move directly from city to country life. He made a wayside stop on Cape Cod where he raised and sold cranberries for a number of years and did various jobs connected with farming and fishing, usually choosing low-paying jobs that no one else wanted. The reason he moved from the city in the first place was a dislike of crowds and what he calls "the usual fate of those in the arts who live in cities." He also notes that the cold climate of Maine is pleasant and stimulating.

Such a simple way of country living is exceptional but by no means as uncommon as one might think. The Enslins' style is certainly not subsistence living (note the music system). With them it has been a matter of choosing the things they really want and sloughing off the non-essentials.

But those choices involve the fact that one must work long hours to live in the country, something that a significant number of people have found makes country life as rough as the city one. The Enslin story illustrates one way to break out of the dawn-to-dusk philosophy which so often has typified country and farm life.

Another profession that can lend itself well to country living is librarianship. I was a professional librarian, for example, for twenty years, and for all that time I lived well out in the country or in small cities or towns. In one job in Ohio, part of my work was to travel with a bookmobile to isolated hamlets and communities.

Generally speaking, librarianship is thought of as an urban-oriented profession, but if one is trained as a librarian and wants to live in the country, one can do it. As with teaching, though, library positions are much scarcer today than five or ten years ago.

While some professions are overcrowded, a rising star is work with the environmental fields. Most prognosticators say that work in these professions is bound to increase, although rather unevenly and at varying rates.

Environmental Activities

Charles Woodard took many ecology courses when he was an undergraduate, and one of his student projects was to establish a nursery for wild trees and bushes. With this experience in his favor, he went to work for the Audubon Society and gained field experience of the most valuable kind. Later, his alma mater decided to institute a program in environmental studies and he was well equipped for the job. Not only did he teach courses in environmental subjects, but he coordinated a number of environmentally-oriented projects such as recycling waste materials and providing for better land use. But these things can be very transitory. His job was phased out after five years.

Marion Metcalf and her son Larry are outstanding amateur ornithologists, mainly self-taught in this exacting discipline. Marion treats her work with birds as a hobby since she has a full-time job, but I'm sure she could earn her entire living from her knowledge of ornithology. At present, Larry is busy with a special bird-banding project and he has held other jobs in this field in the recent past. Neither Marion nor Larry has the degrees in ornithology which would qualify them for professional work, but they do have that exceptional skill, derived from devoted interest in the subject, that easily would qualify them as technicians.

The Center for Northern Studies is, I think, a unique way of making a living in the country. Dr. Steven B. Young, presently in Alaska carrying out a detailed survey under contract with the National Park Service, founded the Center as a private, non-profit organization for education and research in problems of the northern environment.

Certain parts of the northeastern United States have a distinct sub-Arctic climate, which makes it possible for Young and his colleagues to conduct studies of northern conditions and their effects on plants, animals, and men without having to go long distances from the metropolitan centers of the East Coast. In addition to the educational work, there are opportunities for the Center to conduct large-scale scientific surveys like the one now in progress in Alaska. People like Larry Metcalf find employment with the Center in congenial professional surroundings, yet right in the midst of the most rural area you could imagine.

Now we could look in more detail at the lives of people who have combined the somewhat unusual areas of

Environmental Work and Dressmaking, Too

There is an increasing demand these days for environmental specialists of *certain* types in work which often lends itself very nicely to rural living. Bob Keir is a good example of one environmental specialty. He is a fish culture technician working for a state department. He investigates fish kills of various types which may have been caused by pollution or disease or for other reasons, and he cooperates with the biologists and other technicians to abate these kills.

Keir also compiles and tabulates statistics on fish-stocking programs and the costs of operating and maintaining the several game fish hatcheries owned and operated by the Fish and Game Department to provide fish in the state's brooks and streams for recreational fishing.

This present job is the latest in a series that Bob has held with the Department over the twenty-seven years he has worked with them. He began in one of the hatcheries in the northern part of the state at a very low annual income. As he became more skilled through study and experience, he worked his way up to be a hatchery manager, the job he held before his promotion to fish culture technician. Before he received this appointment, he studied at the Eastern Fish Disease Laboratory in Leetown, West Virginia, which primarily is engaged in research under the management of the U.S. Bureau of Sport Fisheries but which does enroll a few students for specialized training in fish culture and disease work. The usual length of the course is six months. In the future most of the special training in this sort of work probably will be done in colleges and universities, and the laboratory in Leetown will be engaged entirely in research.

Although most of Bob's working life has been spent in the field of fish culture, he has held jobs as a firefighter, in the furniture industry, and in the plumbing trade. In college he studied hotel management but decided it was not what he really enjoyed.

Looking back over his work experience, he feels that he made a good choice, since this sort of work has enabled him to spend a good deal of time outdoors and has made it possible for him and his wife, Gladys, to live and raise their three children in a rural environment. The modest pay scale has made it difficult at times for them to make ends meet, but they have been happy and content with their lot.

Gladys Keir has a small business of her own in their home as a professional dressmaker specializing in custom tailoring and sewing. This is a recent development, and she began it because they had just bought an old farmhouse and ten acres of land. To make the house liveable required extensive and costly alterations, so she thought she could use her skill in dressmaking to help pay for their expenses.

Gladys learned sewing from her mother and always has enjoyed needlecraft, so her present business is a natural outgrowth. She tries to spend an eight-hour day exclusively in her sewing room, but even then cannot keep up with the orders.

When she first started business, she advertised in the local paper but soon had to cancel it because she was getting too much work. She could have hired in outside help but prefers to do the work herself and to keep her business accounting as simple as possible.

Although Mrs. Keir does most of her work in one crowded room, she says an ideal work space would have three rooms. The main area where most of the sewing and cutting out is done should have at least twelve by fourteen feet of floor space. The other two rooms could be about nine by nine — one to use for pressing and the other for fitting. The equipment inventory, of course, should have at the head of the list a very good sewing machine. In addition, there should be a cutting table three feet by

eight feet, some full-length mirrors, dress racks, drawers for storing patterns and material, and the usual assortment of scissors, thread, and needles.

Since her business is quite new, she cannot give an accurate prediction of what average annual *net* income might be. But she thinks she isn't charging enough for her work. This is partly because she is just getting her business underway and she finds it difficult to do a thorough cost analysis. She suggests a three to four hundred dollars monthly gross income as a general figure to aim for.

Wildlife Management

The Keirs' oldest son, James, also has decided to go into an aspect of wildlife management work. He has an undergraduate degree from the University of Maine and is completing graduate study at the University of Wisconsin.

But job prospects in wildlife management are not promising.

He is a top student and has a good bit of field experience; yet he is having to search high and low to locate work — any kind of work — in this field. He has written to the wildlife agencies in all of the fifty states, to the Canadian provinces, and to other countries. The replies he gets read, "Your qualifications are excellent, but we just don't have any openings."

The wildlife management branch of environmental work, then, is one to approach gingerly and only after a good deal of consultation with guidance counselors or specialty employment officers. A good agency to find any current openings is Ecology Placement Service which advertises environmental jobs nationwide. Their monthly bulletin (see bibliography) is rather expensive.

Bob's work as a fish hatchery manager has prepared him to run his own private enterprise, and I asked him whether he had ever considered the possibility. He had, but considering the large capital investment needed and the fact that he already has a substantial equity in the state retirement plan, he was reluctant to take the step. Another telling point is the fact that he really enjoys his present work.

A privately-owned fish hatchery and rearing business might be just the ticket for someone, though, for I know of several who seem to be doing a good business. Bob says at present there is an unlimited market for disease-free trout eggs. Restaurant-served trout, also, mostly come from Colorado.

The prime requirement for this business is a good source of water, either from excellent natural springs or from wells that are free of contamination and that produce seven to eight hundred gallons per minute on a regular basis. If the source requires pumping, there is an absolute necessity for an alternative power source in case the regular supply should fail. Any diminution of the water flow would be disastrous. If wells have to be drilled, installing such a water source probably would require a minimum of $40,000. And, as well drillers freely admit, there is no guarantee of what wells will produce, so the water element can be quite a gamble. In addition to the water supply, there will have to be tanks of various sizes (fiberglass is said to be good for this) and at least one good-sized building, plus various pieces of apparatus.

Bob thinks that the total capital investment for an economically-feasible trout hatchery would be at least $100,000 nowadays. That's a large investment and not one to be considered lightly, but for a person willing to study this specialty in all aspects and to take some risks, it could be an attractive way of making a living in the country. A way of expanding the business would be to rear the trout to a size and offer the public the opportunity to angle for them for a fee.

Bradford Angier's *One Acre and Security* (see bibliography) gives a much lower cost estimate for constructing a trout hatchery, and you might like to read what he says about it. Bob Keir says that the best general text on the types of fishes that are raised for sport angling is H. S. Davis's *Culture and Diseases of Game Fishes* (Berkeley, Calif.: University of California Press, 1953).

Another type of fish culture widely practiced in the southern states is called catfish farming. Here the catfish are raised for the most part in man-made ponds until they reach a size for market. Apparently this is quite a good business.

The Agricultural Experiment Station at the University of Georgia in Athens publishes a free book called *Synopsis of Catfish Farming* (Bulletin 69). Then there's the organization called Catfish Farmers of America, located in the Tower Building in Little Rock, Arkansas, 72201, which has membership scattered through the states of Arkansas, Louisiana, Mississippi, and Texas. They publish a newsletter and a journal entitled "The Catfish Farmer".

Certain types of environmental projects and activities *do* need recruits, and one should make great efforts to find the openings. In addition to the sources and references noted above, Odom Fanning has done a good deal of research into vocational openings in the ecological and related fields. The May 1973 issue of *Environmental Quarterly Magazine* carried his article "Job Hunting? Try the Environment." More detailed and thorough, but not so up-to-date, is his full-length book, *Opportunities in Environmental Careers*, (1971), by Vocational Guidance Manuals at 235 East 45th Street, New York, New York, 10017, for $5.75 — or it may be consulted in some libraries.

Art

One definition of an artist is a person who combines the details of human experience into pleasing relationships. But pleasing to whom? If you are an artist and expect to make a living by selling your art to the public, you will have to be something of a market analyst as well as an artist. However, some have graciously combined the two talents.

A friend who used to teach studio art in New Hampshire now has moved on to be an independent artist with two galleries. In the winter he works in Florida and in the summer he opens a Colorado gallery. Has he been successful? I can't give details other than the fact that he's still doing it, and this must be a reasonable criterion of success.

Another artist is Grace Brigham who is an ardent devotee of country living, even though it is rumored that she was born in Brooklyn, New York. Her exquisite skill in drawing with pencil, pen and ink, and in other media, and her talents in illustrating have given her extra income to supplement her teaching art in a rural school.

Dennis Murphy is a musician-artist whose specialty is fabricating musical instruments out of the most unlikely material. He, his wife Pat, and their two daughters live way out in the country where he fashions his unique wind and string instruments, combining this business with teaching music at a nearby college. Pat adds to the family income by working in the college library.

Joan Trimble Smith is an outstanding artist whose specialty is portraits — mostly of children. She and her husband Rob live on the outskirts of Boston in an area that recently has become more metropolitan than rural. But she finds this to be an ideal place to practice her art, for her work relates somewhat to the itinerant artists who used to travel in the country making portraits, sketches, and landscape drawings.

Artists and craftsmen are close kin — so close that sometimes it's futile to attempt separate definitions. Is a potter an artist or a craftsman? What about a blacksmith? Perhaps most people would flinch at the idea of a blacksmith being an artist — or even a craftsman. Nevertheless, I head Orien Dunne's vignette with the title

Artists in Iron

Far from being obsolete, the blacksmith's trade still thrives although it is somewhat altered from yesteryear. In the horse-drawn era the blacksmith-farrier was in constant demand to keep the work horses shod. Then, as motor vehicles took the place of horses, the blacksmith had to look for other ways to make a living. Many of them left the forge and anvil forever while others (Orien Dunne an example) trimmed their sails to the prevailing winds to keep their businesses alive.

Orien Dunne's father was a blacksmith before him, so he learned the trade at home. In the northern community where he lives a lot of lumbering was done in the early part of this century, so he did much traveling from one logging camp to another to shoe the horses. As lumbering declined, Dunne still had enough business taking care of farm horses until the nineteen-forties when tractors became almost universal.

He left blacksmithing for a while and spent a number of years manning a fire lookout tower and doing odd jobs, one of which was operating an elevator in Manhattan. But he missed the blacksmith's trade, and at the earliest opportunity he set up shop again in his native town — as a matter of fact, right on the homestead where he was born and in a new shop he built himself.

Dunne had learned that although blacksmith-farriers no longer were in demand in his region, there was a good opportunity to make ornamental ironwork and various functional implements. So his specialty became custom work on projects brought in by his customers, while he made a few regular items to keep in stock.

In the latter category, heavy sellers are barbecue forks, fireplace tools, sheet-iron baskets for holding fireplace wood, door latches, and chandeliers. He has trouble keeping up with the demand and is using up his inventory of horseshoes by making them into andirons for fireplaces.

From time to time Dunne also makes his own version of the Franklin stove and he keeps a sample of this product in his shop to heat it in the wintertime, since the forge fire isn't sufficient to keep the place comfortable in sub-zero weather.

Mr. Dunne, being in his seventies, has Social Security payments as part of his income. He does the blacksmith work mainly because he really enjoys it, and he doesn't encourage business by advertising except for a small sign on his shop. He takes a relaxed attitude towards his work and will turn down jobs readily if he doesn't approve of them on esthetic grounds. A piece has to be functional, too, or he won't make it.

Dunne makes an important point about earning a living today by blacksmith work. He is convinced that an eager and enthusiastic person working full-time easily could support a family of four quite well indeed. And several blacksmiths besides Mr. Dunne seem to have good businesses, which supports the belief.

Although the number of work horses certainly has declined, there still is an excellent demand for blacksmith-farriers in districts where horseback riding is a favorite recreation. For a young and vigorous person, farriery combined with general blacksmithing indeed could be a good source of income if the area has a number of public or private riding stables. General farriery today requires that the outfit be mobile so that the farrier and his tools can go from place to place as jobs become available.

Today it would cost about five hundred dollars to buy the basic tools needed for general blacksmith work, though sometimes they can be found cheaper at country auctions or at private sales. Added to this would be the expense of building a shop or adapting a building to make it suitable for the forge. Then there would be the cost of an inventory of iron and fuel for the forge.

As many country enterprises go these days, this is a fairly small investment and certainly worth looking into. Some have claimed that blacksmithing is bad for the health because of the smoke, dust and fumes, but Dunne doesn't agree with this at all. He points to himself as one whose health has not suffered from practically a full lifetime at the forge and anvil.

Blacksmithing is learned best by doing, and serving as an apprentice to a master blacksmith is the fundamental way to become proficient. Dunne, who has an apprentice spending a few months from his college career learning the trade, thinks five months sufficient to learn the fundamentals. From then on, it is a matter of perfecting basic skills and improving craftsmanship.

Since a blacksmith-farrier needs to know more than iron, knowledge of horses and horsemanship and also some rudiments of veterinary medicine are essential. He usually attends a school to prepare himself for the business, and County Extension offices can supply details on such schools around the country.

A couple of years ago the fee for shoeing a riding horse was twelve dollars — sometimes more for special corrective shoes. A man can shoe about six horses a day comfortably, and some can do more. This is good country income, but it's hard work and requires considerable strength and a way with horses.

While on the subject of learning a country craft or trade, let me mention the Northeast Center for Cultural Research, Development and Education, a new organization in Maine planned to teach the old crafts through an apprenticeship program. Details on this can be had by writing to the Department of Economic Development in Augusta, Maine.

But let's get back to Orien Dunne once more, for he has another interesting way of supplementing income. In addition to his blacksmith skills, he has considerable knowledge of the old ways of working with wood. He can hew a square timber out of a round log with the broadaxe; split shakes or shingles out of wood bolts with the old-fashioned froe. He also can bore holes lengthwise in logs to make water conduits called pump logs.

Although these skills are not in demand nowadays for practical reasons, Dunne makes twenty-five dollars a day exhibiting these old methods at country fairs where pump log boring, log hewing, and similar handicraft demonstrations are very popular.

Orien Dunne's story and his work indicate clearly how the older trades and crafts can be altered to suit the times.

Emily Bergman and her husband not only have joined their hands in matrimony but also in their crafts. She as a potter works in clay, while her husband works in iron, and they got it all together with wax. It was making and selling candles that earned them the money to set up their present craft establishment.

Mrs. Bergman says it took about five hundred dollars to set up her pottery, while her husband's blacksmith shop, purchased with its tools, cost four hundred dollars. They also bought a house and four acres of land for six thousand dollars.

That's a lot of candles, and though they did have some other money, it wasn't much. It is interesting, incidentally, how close the cost estimates are on the blacksmith enterprises of Dunne and Bergman; yet the two establishments are very distant from one another.

Perhaps the most interesting account of making a living in the country comes from the Gilbertsons who live in Alaska. Though this story is placed in the section on arts and crafts, it might just as well have been included with the part called Working for Wages. It's here because of Pam Gilbertson and her unique business of utilizing native materials in her work. See what the Gilbertsons have to say about

Life in the Alaskan Bush

Bob and Pam Gilbertson live in the Alaskan bush near the south-central village of Cantwell at the edge of Mt. McKinley National Park. Neither of them has a specific year-in, year-out job, but they do all sorts of interesting things to make a living.

In 1972 when they responded to our questionnaire, Bob was earning $1,220 per month as a heavy-equipment operator working for the Alaska Highway Department, his employment guaranteed for six months of the year. In addition to the cash income there are some fringe benefits included with the job.

Pam's Alaskan business license (which cost twenty-five dollars)

enables her to sell to tourists and gift shops her artwork, which consists of pressed wildflower pictures and fur collages. Recently she has taught herself to spin dog hair into yarn, and this she uses to make warm and beautiful hats, mittens, and sweaters. There is a great demand for her product both from Alaskans and tourists.

And there is a good deal of satisfaction for the Gilbertsons in having figured out a way to use a by-product from their team of sled dogs. The loose undercoat of dog fur otherwise would have been wasted if Pam had not thought of this unique use. She grossed $2,000 the first year in sales of her products and having set herself up in business, she can deduct certain expenses from gross income.

The Gilbertsons point out that one of the keys to success for life in Alaska (and particularly out in the bush) is to be a "jack-of-all-trades." Bob, in addition to the highway employment, has part-time income of slightly over five dollars an hour working as the need arises for the Alaska State Police as jailer. He also is trained as an emergency medical technician and ambulance driver and is on call for volunteer ambulance duty.

He does odd jobs, besides, in construction and mechanical work for Cantwell community members, getting five to six dollars per hour. Other sidelines have included being a herder for the University of Alaska Reindeer Research Station in Cantwell, truck driver, mechanic's helper, and doing general construction for the National Park Service. Income from these sources has ranged from about six to nine dollars per hour, and overtime makes a significant difference, boosting the hourly rate considerably.

Alaskan employment opportunities are very seasonal in nature, and one has to consider wintertime as a low point in the job curve. But by careful management and some assistance from unemployment checks, the Gilbertsons have lived on about three hundred and twenty dollars a month in the winter and have not had to call on their savings.

In mid-1973 I asked the Gilbertsons how much they thought it would require annually for a family of four to live in Alaska. Pam replied, "This is a difficult question to answer with so many "ifs" involved. The best I can do is to let you know how much we feel we could live comfortably on if we had two children, lived in Cantwell at our present location, and maintained our current interests. In that case we would consider $14,000 per year an adequate income. A family could live on less, however, if willing to forego the modern conveniences of electricity, oil heat and cooking with gas. The less equipment you have to maintain, the cheaper your living costs, and there are certainly many families living in the Alaskan bush who choose this way. Naturally, it's more fun to live with less out of choice rather than necessity! Yearly income would vary, of course, in different localities in Alaska. In general, we've found you can live cheaper in the bush than in a city because much less emphasis is put on luxuries."

Pam and Bob get a lot of satisfaction from their varied work routine and find that each day is a new experience, offering variety and challenge to their lives. Bob writes, "The things we do each day to survive are the things that make life interesting and exciting. We know why we are alive and it is because of what we accomplish with our own hands and minds — not depending on anyone else."

The fact that Bob has a degree in forestry and has held a wide range of different jobs in the lower forty-eight undoubtedly has contributed to his successful adjustment to the extremely difficult Alaskan employment situation. Although he does not seem to be using his specific professional forestry training in Alaska, this type of educational background could have many indirect advantages in a frontier-like environment. Bob also has worked with all sorts of mechanical devices ranging from lathes, drill presses, and caterpillar tractors, all the way to electronic computers. Familiarity with such a variety of equipment could not but be helpful when it comes to repairing an electric generator in the backwoods or in getting an ambulance started at forty below zero. Pam's background in art work, correspondingly, has prepared her to take advantage of the opportunities to design unique and beautiful things from native materials. In addition to their schooling and training, both Pam and Bob, it is apparent, are well endowed with good common sense and basic intelligence.

Before they left for Alaska, the Gilbertsons had $3,000 in savings, a new four-wheel drive station wagon, and a six-by-six by ten-foot homemade trailer. They sold everything they thought would not be needed in their new life in Alaska and packed the remainder, including three dogs, into the wagon and trailer.

Their financial assets included the value of their vehicle and the trailer. They figured it cost them six hundred dollars to travel from Minneapolis to Anchorage via the Alcan highway.

What is most important to any family planning a new life in Alaska, they had the assurance of employment when they arrived on the scene. Bob's first job in Cantwell consisted of running a bar and cafe, managing a grocery store, a service station and bulk plant. Then as now he took on part-time jobs, such as plowing snow and hauling wild game. Pam was able to earn two dollars an hour helping out in the store and cafe from time to time. Bob's income from this first job was $1,000 a month.

They had to pay rental of one hundred dollars a month, plus utilities, to get living space in a two-bedroom ten by forty-five foot trailer. But on this first job they were able to save out several hundred dollars a month because they had little time or opportunity to spend money. They worked long hours and it was hard work, but the varied routine suited them then as it does now; each day being an event in itself.

The Gilbertsons' objective in coming to Alaska was not to live in a village and get rich. At the first opportunity, and with a good deal of luck, they were able to rent at thirty-five dollars a month a five-room cabin on five acres of land two miles from the village of Cantwell. Purchase of Alaskan land not only is almost impossible, but it's very expensive. At the time the Gilbertsons were looking for a place of their own, people were asking two thousand dollars an acre for land in their remote area.

Although it would seem that such a thinly-populated place as Alaska with such a huge land area would be filled with chances to buy land, this is just not the case. It's because of land claims settlements and the enormous tracts owned by the state and federal governments, and what private land is on the market goes at inflated prices.

There is some "open-to-entry" land available in Alaska but it lies in extremely remote areas where access is difficult and there are virtually no employment opportunities. After the native corporations have selected their land and have decided what to do with it, the situation may change. But this will take some time. In 1974 it's not just a simple thing to go to Alaska and get a dream place for a song.

The Gilbertsons were fortunate in their location, for they really do live out in the bush, yet are not too far from a community and places of employment. They don't earn from their land except as Pam uses wildflowers, fur, and other native things for her art work. However, a major part of their meat and fish does come from the forests and streams. Bob and Pam also collect wild berries and rose hips to add variety to their meals and they intend to make even more use of the numerous edible wild plants which grow there in summertime.

Gardening, particularly near Cantwell, is practically impossible because of the high latitude, 2,200-foot elevation, and cool weather in summer. The Gilbertsons do intend to build an artificially-heated greenhouse sometime, and this will provide them with some fresh vegetables of the smaller sort.

Other more temperate zones of Alaska are excellent for general gardening and farming. The Matanuska Valley, the region northeast of Anchorage, and parts of the Kenai Peninsula are examples. Other and more unusual garden enterprises in Alaska are well described in Frances W. Townley's "Gardens Under the Arctic Sun" in the June 1973 issue of *Organic Gardening and Farming*.

Some people who went to Alaska on a tour a few years ago told me they paid a dollar and twenty-five cents for a flimsy peanut butter sandwich. Pam says the reason for this is because of high labor costs. Groceries in Anchorage and Fairbanks are not much higher than in Minneapolis, and in fact some are cheaper.

When the Gilbertsons first came to Cantwell, there was no road and it was impossible to drive to Anchorage, but now the road is finished and they drive there about four times a year, spending several hundred dollars stocking up on groceries in case lots. But they buy only enough meat to give a change from the usual diet of wild game.

An important point about living in the bush is to be sure there are alternative facilities available. As Bob says, ". . . we have our cabin organized like a space ship. We try to have a 'back-up system' for everything. Our power plant is a necessity only in the summertime for refrigeration — in winter that's no problem. We have kerosene lamps and candles. Batteries are kept handy, too. I devised a hand pump system valved into the water system, and we have an outhouse for the times we're short of water. The oil furnace requires no electricity but works on a gravity, hot air system. Even so, we have a wood stove standing by and a supply of wood cut."

Bob and Pam say that they don't have any long-range goals. They like to live each day for itself and enjoy life as it flows on. Bob works long hours when employment is available. Pam works at home on her art designs and sales. They have no children. Their leisure is taken up in the near vicinity of their home in the bush. A team of sled dogs provides dependable winter transportation and is a source of enjoyment, as they both are extremely fond of dogs.

Although the Gilbertsons find that making a living in the Alaskan bush suits them to a tee, they emphasize that it's an extremely difficult life, laden with pitfalls which inexperienced people find most disconcerting. Especially interesting is Pam's opinion on how women get along in Alaska, as we always think of it as a man's country. The answer, of course, is that if a woman really desires to go to Alaska and live in the bush, she is perfectly capable of doing so and enjoying herself every bit as much as a man. Pam says, "I could go on indefinitely about a woman's place here in the Alaskan bush and what things a woman can learn to love here, but that would take hours and it's a project I would have to save for winter!"

Good health, stamina, resourcefulness and inventiveness are qualities that are useful anywhere in the country. In the Alaskan bush they are essential to survival. Bob writes, "One mistake with the wind chill factor at one hundred and forty below zero can kill you. We are more than two hundred miles from our supply points. We can't go to town to buy a 'widget' to fix or build something any old time. We have wolves, grizzly bears and angry momma moose for neighbors. The bush is beautiful but dangerous. Nevertheless, here we feel alive and useful not only to ourselves but to others in the community as well. We've found our niche."

Crafts

Erlend Jacobsen started out as a college professor and then went into a full-time business of making candles. It's an everlasting amazement to me how candle-making could be so profitable, but I'm persuaded it is by reading that not only has Mr. Jacobsen done well at it but "175,000 customers buy from the Candle Mill in East Arlington, Vermont, annually." This is quoted of Tom Weakley's popular book, *How to Make Candles*.

Kitchen Candlecrafting by Ruth Monroe has some very pertinent suggestions about setting up a small shop, in addition to the text on actual candle making. All in all, I would say that the chandler's craft is far from defunct and a very likely prospect for a

country business. If you are thinking of making a living from candle sales, though, be sure to do a market analysis beforehand.

Retirement Income

Una Yahkub does very well at a country craft of making dolls from corn husks. She learned how years ago when she was a youngster brought up in the Appalachian highlands, but it was only after she had retired from teaching that she turned back to this unusual craft. This is not her principal way of making a living, since she and her husband have retirement income, but she finds the money she earns is much more than expected, and it gives the

Yahkubs something extra for special things. Like many crafts, this making of corn husk dolls could be considered a way of making a partial income to supplement wage labor or retirement income.

Learning how to become a craftsman is not so difficult now as it was ten years ago, for a resurgence of interest in crafts seems to have swept the country. Much of this is the result of the younger generation's disillusionment with an increasingly complex and barren technology which did not seem to offer a real sense of personal fulfillment. With craft work a person can shape raw materials into unique, beautiful and useful things, and with a minimum of time and equipment. Much craft work is undertaken, also, as a sort of personal therapy, with no idea that whatever is made should be sold.

Along with this is the desire among buyers to have hand-fashioned things of beauty and utility in their homes. It is from this tendency that the craftsman who wants to make a living from his craft can benefit. If he has not learned this skill at home, then he has many opportunities to learn it in colleges, schools, adult education classes, and apprenticeships.

As you read in Orien Dunne's story, he delights in being able to pass on his skill in ironwork and woodworking to younger people. And the Holmes family in Maine is particularly eager to see that the apprenticeship method gets off to a good start. See what they have to say about this in

Woodcraft Down East

I never thought of Cape Cod as particularly metropolitan, but Mr. and Mrs. David J. Holmes thought it was and moved to Maine to escape the urban sort of existence that is making the Cape a hectic place to live and to have their children grow up where they could raise animals and learn responsibility.

The Holmes sold their place on Cape Cod, using the money to purchase a 260-acre farm in Maine. They didn't have quite enough to pay for their new place completely, so the former owner agreed to hold a small mortgage for the balance, and gave them a year to get started before making payments.

Mr. Holmes is a woodcarver, and the sale of his work requires that their place be accessible to customers. This was taken into consideration when they selected their new home which is near major highways and is centrally located in the state, although it is truly in the country, on top of a hill with a gorgeous view. They are satisfied that they made the right choice to move to this new environment, even though it has entailed a lot of work.

Mr. Holmes attended a private school, a military academy, had one year at the Massachusetts Maritime Academy and one year of college; Mrs. Holmes has a high school education and a Massachusetts hairdresser's license.

David Holmes' natural ability in the art field led to his becoming a woodcarver, and he had a successful business on Cape Cod. While income from the carving business is their major source of support, Mrs. Holmes helps out the finances with part-time jobs such as a Head Start nurse's aide, a summer job in a restaurant, and a stint of jury duty. However, she has found that she can "make" more money by staying at home and helping her husband with the finishing of his products as his business and reputation grow.

In 1970 Holmes took a fifteen-week course in New Hampshire to learn all the aspects of being a sawyer, in order to run the sawmill they purchased with a loan through the Farm Home Administration. This they set up on their property to cut wood for the carvings and for buildings they are constructing. The next year they cut the lumber on their sawmill to add a two-and-a-half story addition to the woodcarving shop.

They have found markets for the woodcarvings and scrimshaw and sculptured whales teeth, for which he takes orders, mainly obtained from signs in banks, restaurants, and tourist homes.

Although their income is somewhat less than before they moved, the Holmes' mode of living does not require a great amount of money. They "work to live" not "live to work." Like many other country folk, they find that a large garden helps on the food bill. Mrs. Holmes preserves the garden harvest for winter use, she makes butter and cheese from the milk of their cow, and they also raise and slaughter for meat the livestock which the four children help to care for. Mrs. Holmes does all the usual household chores like washing, ironing, mending and making clothes, and even finds some time for interior decoration of their 153-year-old farmhouse. She also makes soap the way it was taught to her by her mother, as were most of the things she does for the family's welfare. The family works together and they travel all over the state of Maine to craft fairs.

David Holmes now has started carving classes at his workshop as a beginning of the Northeast Center for Cultural Research, Development and Education. This long-worked-for non-profit project is intended to teach the old crafts through an apprenticeship program. The project is coming along slowly, but without any outside financial aid.

In spite of much hard work, the Holmes' enthusiasm for the country life hasn't been dampened and they continue to live and practice a philosophy of simplicity.

Products From the Land

In most people's minds the most obvious way of making a living in the country is to be a farmer, either by growing vegetable crops or livestock or both, and then selling these for income, while retaining a portion for home use.

Farming

One of the most successful farm families in my experience are the Ferrises who operate a dairy farm in the upland country. Bob Ferris, being most alert to rapidly changing farm conditions, always has modified his herd and equipment to take advantage of improvements in dairy technology. It's always a pleasure to visit the Ferris farm, to see the spotless milk room and carefully tilled fields and healthy cattle. The mark of success is all over the place. This is a monument to a lifetime of hard work and unrelenting

attention every day of the year. And it's by just such continuous application of effort that dairy farmers keep solvent.

To get started in dairying requires a considerable capital investment in land, buildings, equipment and stock. In order to have a decent income from a dairy herd means that the farmer should be milking at least forty cows morning and night. Probably $75,000 would be the minimum needed, and this is one of the reasons we haven't gone into so many details about getting into this occupation.

On the other hand, another kind of farm family has only two cows and some poultry, makes some income from selling the milk direct to customers who come to pick it up, and derives more from the sale of fresh eggs. This type of small-scale farming combined with another source of income, such as wage labor, probably is more appropriate to the reader of this book than intensive commercial farming of the kind carried on by the Ferris family.

A small general farm should be quite diversified and be aimed more towards being self-sufficient than toward being a large income producer.

I think that the small, diversified general farm can offer more satisfaction to the owners than would a large-scale operation. Most county agents would say that I am foolish to recommend such a plan, but they generally are trained in the principles of agribusiness, so it's natural for them to think along these lines.

Here are two cases to support my view. In the first story you will see how Charles Sanders supplemented his general farming routine with forestry work. This is a study in

Yankee Ingenuity

So many interesting types of work are connected with the woodlands that a whole book could be devoted to forest occupational specialties. Only a few of them are woodlands culture and management; managing woodlands as playgrounds for hiking, fishing, hunting, et cetera; firefighters and smokewatchers; wardens of various types maintaining security in the forests; maintenance people who keep the woodland roads and bridges in repair; dendrologists who study the botany of trees; woodland surveyors who establish property lines and bounds; and a whole array of people who are concerned with harvesting woodland products.

Charles Sanders illustrates the type of person who combines woods work with general farming to make a living in the country. Although now of retirement age, he is as busy as ever working full days year in and year out. He does this because he enjoys it and would be unhappy if he couldn't get outside every day. His wife is dead and his family grown up (although many of them are living nearby).

He moved onto the farm where he is living now about 1935, buying the buildings and land by using life insurance as collateral. In large part he paid for the farm and supported his family by harvesting firewood and logs from the extensive woodlands. Yet in the 'thirties firewood was selling for only about seven dollars a cord, delivered to a village five miles away. He also cut logs and sold to a local sawmill until he purchased his own mill and sawed out lumber himself.

In addition to the woods work, Sanders tended his farm animals and crops. His specialty was dairying (about twenty cows to be milked). At one time he had some three hundred hogs, but this business was destroyed by a livestock quota system established during World War II. At another time he tried raising turkeys and although he was successful in getting a flock established, the market for these birds wasn't profitable enough for him to continue.

He earned money, too, by hiring out with his team of horses to other farms for spring and summer work. His wife and growing family helped with the chores and with the multitude of other things that have to be done on a farm. He also exchanged labor with the neighbors in barter so that neither of the parties had to pay cash for wages. To catalog fully the variety of jobs he has done at one time or another would take several pages. The main point his life illustrates, however, is the need for a rural person to be very adaptable and capable and willing to do a great diversity of work. And another point his life emphasizes is that he has never totally relied on one form of income-producer. As the old adage says: it's foolish to put all your eggs in one basket.

The success pattern of the very small farmer almost always is typified by versatility. It often includes working part-time in factories or shops when this work is available. But even with the best of application and hard work, jacks of many trades have a difficult time keeping solvent, for the U.S. economic market favors the agricultural giants at the expense of the small operator.

In 1972 Sanders bought his second sawmill, but this time it was more to have for a hobby than for necessity. It is a good used mill powered with a stationary diesel engine. To go with the mill he also purchased a flat-bed truck for hauling logs and lumber and a crawler tractor to get logs out of the woods.

These items of second-hand equipment, combined with some already on hand (such as a chain saw, sleds and scoots, peavies, and chains) make it possible for him not only to harvest the trees but to cut them into boards, planks and timbers ready for use in the building trades. He prefers to buy the logs as living trees (stumpage, as it is called), fell the trees, haul them to the mill, and saw out the lumber. This is more profitable than custom sawing where the customer brings his own logs to the mill to be converted into lumber. By keeping his business small enough to be operated by himself, he can avoid a lot of involved bookkeeping and payroll data, and he does not get involved with the complicated provisions of the Federal Occupational Safety and Health Act, outlined in detail under the story of Maurice Page.

Another branch of the wood products business which Sanders has gone into is harvesting and marketing fence posts of white cedar, which is very good for the purpose because it is resistant to decay.

Often posts are set in post holes with the butts down to eliminate frost heaving, but in the stoney region where Mr. Sanders lives, it is exceedingly difficult to dig. Therefore, he tapers the small ends of the posts so that they can be driven with a maul, and he delivers his sharpened posts to individual farmers or to farm equipment dealers.

The fence post market always is good wherever there is livestock to be fenced in, and Sanders considers this one of his more successful activities. The business has a peak in the springtime when farmers need the posts to repair the fences from winter damage, and to take advantage of this seasonal market he tries to have a good inventory on hand.

Pulpwood for paper manufacture is another Sanders forest product. Spruce and fir trees (and now hardwoods, also) too small for logs are harvested in four-foot lengths and sold by the cord to the paper mills or to jobbers. Like many others, this business has its ups and downs, and a person who owns trees suitable for pulpwood must be alert to market conditions. One can get valuable help, however, from his county forester who can advise what trees should be cut, whether for pulpwood or other markets, and when to cut them.

The hardwood firewood Mr. Sanders once sold for seven dollars a cord today fetches forty dollars and more. The wood must be cut to shorter lengths, however — eighteen or twenty-four inches for fireplace wood and twelve to sixteen inches for stove wood — and be split.

Economists in the heavily-forested states are predicting that wood as a fuel may be used on a large scale again, this time in wood-burning electric generating stations. Much of the nation's forestland is growing up to types of trees that can be utilized best as fuel. If the cutting is done on a selective basis and according to sound forestry practices, this could result in more productive woodlands and at the same time decrease the demand for non-renewable fossil fuels.

If this development should take place, there would be even more markets for fuel wood from privately owned forests, and it would provide another quite dependable source of income for the countryman. Clever folks like Charles Sanders will keep this possibility in mind.

Market Gardening

Another very important source of income from the land is in selling fresh vegetables from a small truck or market garden. This is very seasonal work, with labor and income concentrated in the growing and harvesting season. However, we are not concerned with the very large truck gardens that ship produce to urban markets. We're talking about the small family-run market garden that grows produce for a local market, either from a roadside stand or in a small city farmer's market.

More often than not, this kind of gardener will offer produce that has been grown on soil that is not heavily dosed with artificial fertilizer. Neither does this gardener apply large quantities of pesticides to the growing crops. In fact many of these gardeners are real purists and will not consider *any* use of chemical fertilizer or *any* artificial pesticides acceptable. Their philosophy has dollar advantages, too, for many people will pay a premium price for produce that has been grown by these so-called organic methods. Generally speaking, small market gardeners have on their side today the advantage that a lot of consumers are unhappy about the packaged produce that is offered in the supermarkets. They often will drive several miles to buy their vegetables fresh from the garden.

This I can cite from my own experience in the extensive vegetable garden I have had for seventeen years. Primarily I grow vegetables for our own use, but from time to time I get over-enthusiastic about peas or corn or spinach or potatoes and have more than we can use. By just dropping a slight hint that I might be willing to sell some of these things, the grapevine gets humming and I have more customers than I can accommodate. Just now I have a surplus of potatoes, and hardly a day goes by that someone doesn't stop to see if he can buy some.

I use this example to suggest home-grown crops as a means of producing income, yet some readers will wonder why, if I like gardening and have plenty of customers, I don't operate a market garden. It's because I have a singular pest that would destroy a large market garden overnight here where I live. This is the white-tailed deer which devours practically anything in the garden unless it's elaborately protected.

The deer in my garden suggest how a potential success story had to be modified. Insect pests are not the least that the gardener has to contend with, for woodchucks and raccoons make their inroads too. The only really effective way of dealing with them is by very expensive and complicated fencing or by twenty-four hour patrols — both of which are too much for me to consider. If you are thinking of market gardening, think not only of your market but also how you can get the crops to marketable size. If you find the solutions, you have much of the answer.

A market garden located on a well-travelled road has the great advantage of allowing direct selling at a roadside stand. Near an automobile assembly plant in rural Ohio, for instance, a number of gardeners found they were in a perfect position to benefit from the workers going home from the plant.

Not all will be in such an ideal situation, though, and if you are thinking about selling garden produce and you live on a lightly travelled road, you might consider taking your produce to market. In quite a number of cities there now are Farmers' Markets that offer space to gardeners in a central location for a small fee. One Farmers' Market not far from my home runs a slow second to roadside stands for perishable produce. Another deterrent is that the farmer or his representative has to be on hand to sell the produce. Of course this is true also for the roadside stand, but often a farmer at his roadside stand can be doing other things nearby while waiting for customers. At the Market there is very little opportunity for productive work while tending a booth. The best-selling products at a Farmers' Market are apt to be home-produced things like herbs, sprouted grains, and non-seasonal items like milled flour, cheeses, honey, maple products and the like.

Another point on Farmers' Markets, apparently a requirement for success, is that the area have a high-density population and be centrally located to allow for a good deal of walk-in trade. Auto mobility clearly favors the roadside market stand on well-travelled highways, especially if these highways carry home-bound commuters.

The most successful roadside vegetable and fruit stands are those that specialize in having crops on sale before anyone else. These early, early vegetables and fruits always command a premium price. One farmer near me used to *net* $2,000 annually on these specialty items over and beyond his regular produce. To do this requires a greenhouse or a combination of hot beds and cold frames. But there's an added possibility here — that of selling started plants to the customers who want them for their own gardens.

Market gardening with sales provided through a roadside stand, combined with a small greenhouse (where the climate requires it) and some general livestock farming, seems to be about the best of all possible ways of making a living in the country if you can circumvent pest problems such as I mentioned above.

Livestock and gardening often are very compatible. I have found it immensely helpful to have several pigs here at my place during the summer season, for they are overjoyed to clean up all sorts of garden wastes, from weeds to thinnings and harvest remainders such as cornstalks. These creatures eat practically anything and although you can fatten them more quickly on prepared feeds, they do well on home produce that otherwise would go to waste.

But if you are thinking of fattening hogs for the commercial market this way, forget it. Pork now falls under very strict regulations and you practically have to give the inspectors the pigs' day-by-day menu if you want to sell them as meat. I was thinking of pork for home consumption.

But to get back to market gardening for a while, let's read about the Harrs and their

Georgian Gardens

It often happens that a nudge from an unexpected source will set off a train of interesting events. In the case of Robert Harrs his layoff from well-paid engineering work at Lockheed in Georgia prompted him and his wife, Celeste, and their five children to do something they always wanted to do — make a living in the country. And their experience has prompted three of their friends to move out into their neighborhood, too, while five more are seriously considering a move. Perhaps an industrial layoff can have compensations other than starting a run on the local welfare office.

The Harrs' first step was to locate property suited to their needs. In 1971 they found a forty-acre piece of land on top of Little Sand Mountain in Armuchee, Georgia. Thirty of the acres were in woodland and the rest arable, and it's said to be the best truck farming area in northwest Georgia.

Although the land was good, not much could be said of the house when they moved in. It had no plumbing, the walls were full of cracks and holes, and there was only one light bulb and a single pot-bellied stove for heat. But the sadly neglected house has responded to their affectionate attentions, and they say that "the old place evokes such a feeling of hominess that we've decided to add onto it and stay here forever."

This real estate cost them $7,500 which they paid for by selling their suburban home. That left them without much capital except money earned in the woodland, which they thinned judiciously. From twenty acres of thinning they were able to sell enough pulpwood to get a truck, some tools and farm implements, a cow and garden supplies.

The next growing season they put in one acre of vegetables for home use, an acre for strawberries, two acres of corn, a couple of acres for watermelons, tomatoes, and other crops. They plan to set out two or three acres into an orchard of fruit and nut trees.

Before the gardening season began their first year, both Robert and Celeste worked at hauling pulpwood, and Robert picked up some extra income operating a bulldozer, as well as having the use of the machine to clear a pasture area. In all their projects they have had help from the children who are old enough. The youngest are three and five; the older ones seventeen, twelve, and nine.

More recently Robert has found work as a project engineer sixteen miles from home, while Celeste manages the homestead operation and gets added income by selling garden produce. They plan to sell substantial amounts of organically grown produce from their several garden plots.

Although their income took a sharp drop when Robert was laid off at Lockheed, it since has recovered almost to the previous point, particularly because of his new job. As income increases

from their garden sales, they will be quite well off financially, not to mention the numerous fringe benefits of country living.

One of the special benefits that the Harrs find in their new neighborhood is that they are respected for the fact that they neither smoke nor drink, while in suburbia they were thought to be kind of oddballs for this conviction.

Although it cannot be taken for granted that country people are more tolerant than city dwellers, they often seem to be. And the advantage of spaciousness in the rural areas is important. At least in the country one is not living cheek by jowl with people and is not pressured to conform to their ways.

My sister, her husband and their children once had a very successful worm business, raising and selling earthworms to fishermen as bait. They are no longer in the business, but the number of roadside signs we see suggests that fishermen still are willing to put down cash for bait.

Here is another part-time income or way to make a living in the country, and though few probably ever make this their total means of income, some who raise earthworms on a large scale have made this their sole means of support.

Bait for fishermen can include a larger variety than worms too — other forms of live bait such as minnows and hellgramites. And then there is the whole realm of artificial lures that can produce income for the person who enjoys tying flies or making spinners.

Raising fish for the market from fresh water ponds, suggested in the earlier account of catfish farming, seems to have considerable potential as a way of making money in the country. Louis Bromfield's account of how he linked the ponds on his farms with a food production cycle is recounted in *Pleasant Valley* and *Malabar Farm*, which also tell more about a rural way of life that you should know about. If you are interested in raising fish as a way of making a living in the country, you will also want to send for the publications mentioned in the Keirs' story (Environmental Work and Dressmaking Too).

Another country business is minerals. By this I don't imply mining or quarrying operations, but the selection, display and sales of semi-precious minerals at a roadside stand. In addition to selling the raw minerals, one could also think about a lapidary shop where one cuts and finishes minerals to beautiful forms. Depending what is found near you, it might be a single specialty. One man takes soapstone (steatite) and makes stoves from this remarkable stone. And then there are the Eskimos who carve soapstone into beautiful sculptures.

One could go on endlessly describing the ways of using products of the land to make a full- or part-time income, but the book then would be more of a cyclopedia and more detailed than the present scope would admit. I would like to hear from readers, however, who have unique ideas and experience or other advice on ways of making a living either *in* or *from* the country, for perhaps we have merely scratched the surface.

When one thinks about all the pleasant things that can be done in the country, it would be nice to apply for an extension of life expectancy so that we could get to those things that there otherwise won't be time for. As one of my collaborators said, "If we're not getting rich, at least we're having a lot of fun."

In Summary

Although it's sometimes dangerous to abbreviate and condense because of oversimplification, nevertheless I'm going to try to put some of the main points involved with making a living in the country here in very short form as a general summary.

I think the first and most important consideration is that people must have a deep-seated wish to be country folk or small town residents. They must love open spaces, fields and forests, running streams, broad lakes, wide skies, wind and weather. If they truly like to have these things around them day in and day out and think of the attendant hardships and inconveniences of a rural existence as minor considerations, then they are pointed in the right direction — given a moderate dollop of good luck, a fair measure of common sense and some organizational skills.

Probably one of the reasons you picked up this book in the first place and have read this far is because you already *have* the real desire to be in the country. I can't help you to beguile Lady Luck, nor can I do much about your common sense. But organizational skills can be communicated to a degree — sometimes even to a high degree — and it's the acquisition and refinement of these skills that will provide a considerable part of one's success story.

If you plan to succeed, it is quite likely that you *will* succeed, despite occasional evidence to the contrary. Your plan of moving to the country will take some time to ripen, so don't be in too much of a hurry about the whole thing, and don't be afraid to change some aspects of the plan along the way as conditions and circumstances themselves change.

So the first step is to have a plan, and a rather detailed one at that. Much of it can be developed in your head, but the more you get out in the open on paper or in conversation with those who are

close to you, the better off everyone will be. It will avoid later disagreement and misunderstandings.

Your plan too, should be in part an inventory of assets and liabilities. For example: are your temperaments suited to the rather independent way of life that making a living in the country usually involves? Some of these needful characteristics are: venturesomeness, innovativeness, persistence and self-discipline — all in a nicely balanced brew.

Are you aware of (and are you constantly seeking out) the many free and inexpensive sources of information and advice? As you learn about new ways and methods of doing things, be flexible to initiate change, yet without being whimsical about it.

When it comes to moving from one place to another, seriously consider the balance between where it's pleasant to be and where the sources of money lie, whether from wage labor or from markets for your products or your services. Further along this line, consider renting for a while before plunking down cash for a down payment and mortgaging your future. Then from your rented location, you can more leisurely look around you to determine if you really can make a go of it there and enjoy it at the same time.

All along the way it pays to stop, look and listen — particularly so in the early stages when you are getting your feet under you.

If you are the vendor of a product or a service, try to make it top quality. Satisfied customers are the best advertising. The quote from Emerson at the front of the book was born of wisdom.

Since low income generally is a reality for most country folk, develop economical habits. Instead of paying cash, try bartering. Renewable resources from the land like food from gardens and fuel from the forests usually are better and cheaper in the long run. Purchase things in bulk whenever possible, possibly dividing large orders with friends and neighbors.

If it seems that some of the case studies in this book are close models for you to follow, be sure that most of the characteristics of the cases fit your own situation.

When you have matured that plan, then you must get your wits about you, take a deep breath and DO IT!

List of References

I have tried to bring together here a fairly wide selection of references for those who are interested in country life. Most are books currently available either in libraries or from bookstores. In a few cases organizations are noted that people may call on and there are some publishers whose catalogs will supplement my list. Many of the books on the list are in print both in hard cover and in paperback versions, and when this is the case, I have given the prices of the paperback editions.

Agricultural Board. QUALITY OF RURAL LIFE. National Academy of Science, 1971. ($2.95)

American Country Life Association. 2118 South Summit Avenue, Sioux Falls, South Dakota 57105.
Representatives of agriculture, education, religion, health and welfare groups and individuals interested in encouraging and promoting a satisfying and wholesome rural life. Originated in the Country Life Movement inaugurated during the administration of President Theodore Roosevelt. Irma E. Herrboldt, Secretary-Treasurer.

Angier, Bradford. ONE ACRE AND SECURITY: HOW TO LIVE OFF THE LAND WITHOUT RUINING IT. Stackpole Books, 1972. ($6.95)
Mr. Angier lists a wide variety of country enterprises: goat and cattle farming; beekeeping; fish, frog and turtle farming; poultry; rabbits; earthworms; herb culture, etc. He also has advice on simple home construction and other topics. I feel he tends to oversimplify the problems attendant on getting started in business, and it seems that many of his cost estimates are too low.

Ayer . . . DIRECTORY OF NEWSPAPERS AND PERIODICALS.
    Ayer, 1973. Revised annually.
Gives essential details on a very large selection of newspapers and
periodicals, with additional gazetteer information on U.S. and
Canadian cities. A library reference book.

Ball, Al. WOOD CARVING FOR FUN AND PROFIT. Exposition
    Press, 1969. ($3.50)

Bealer, Alex W. ART OF BLACKSMITHING. illus. Funk &
    Wagnalls, 1969. ($10.00)

Bolles, Richard N. WHAT COLOR IS YOUR PARACHUTE?
    Box 4310, Berkeley, California 94704. Ten Speed Press.
The author deals with an individual's use of his skills. A career can
be thought of as how these skills are used in various combinations
through a lifetime.

BOOKS IN PRINT: an author-title-series index to the PUBLISH-
    ERS' TRADE LIST ANNUAL. Bowker, 1973. Revised an-
    nually.
Enables one to locate available books either by author or title and
gives ordering information. A library reference book.

Borsodi, Ralph. FLIGHT FROM THE CITY: AN EXPERIMENT
    IN CREATIVE LIVING ON THE LAND. Harper-Row, 1972.
    ($1.95)

Bromfield, Louis. MALABAR FARM. Ballantine Books, 1971.
    ($1.95)

Bromfield, Louis. PLEASANT VALLEY. Ballantine, 1970. ($1.25)
I had the pleasant opportunity to visit Mr. Bromfield's experiment
in country living in Mansfield, Ohio and can vouch for the fact that
his farms were everything he described so well in these two books.
The farms are maintained today as Mr. Bromfield hoped they would
be — as examples of productive country living.

CANADIAN ALMANAC AND DIRECTORY. Copp, Clark, 1973.
    Revised annually.

Comprehensive data on legal, commercial, statistical, astronomical, departmental, ecclesiastical, financial and educational topics. A library reference book.

Coleman, Donald G. WOODWORKING FACT BOOK: BASIC INFORMATION ON WOOD FOR WOOD CARVERS, HOME WOODSHOP CRAFTSMEN, TRADESMEN AND INSTRUCTORS. illus. Speller. ($15.00)

Eckert, John E. & Shaw, Frank R. BEEKEEPING. illus. Macmillan, 1960. ($12.50)
I can recommend this book highly.

Ecology Placement Service: advertises environmental jobs nationwide. A monthly bulletin of current offerings. 1711 Lincoln. St. Paul, Minnesota 55105. $6.00 per month. $11.00 for two months. $16.00 for three months.

ENCYCLOPEDIA OF ASSOCIATIONS. 7th ed. Gale Research Co., 1972. 3 volumes.
"A guide to national and international organizations including: trade, business and commercial; agricultural and commodity; governmental, public administration, military and legal; scientific, engineering and technical; educational and cultural; social welfare; health and medical; public affairs; fraternal, foreign interest, nationality and ethnic; religious; horticultural; veterans; hereditary and patriotic; hobby and avocational; athletic and sports; labor unions; chambers of commerce; Greek letter; and general (unclassified)". Volume 2 is a geographic and executive index. Volume 3 lists new associations and projects on a quarterly basis. A library reference book.

Examinations and Home Study. The National Learning Corp. 20 Du Pont Street, Plainview, New York 11803.
This company publishes manuals for specific preparation in various professional, sub-professional and technical occupations in addition to the popular Civil Service Examination Passbook series.

Extension Service. A nationwide organization of agricultural, forestry and home economics experts supported by tax dollars through the U.S. Department of Agriculture and the State Agricultural Colleges. There is an office of the extension service in each county seat. Look in your phone book for their number. The extension service distributes, mostly free of charge, a great variety of publications of considerable interest and value to country folk.

Fanning, Odom. JOB HUNTING? TRY THE ENVIRONMENT. In: Environmental Quality Magazine. Volume 4, Number 5. May 1973. pp. 51ff.

Fanning, Odom. OPPORTUNITIES IN ENVIRONMENTAL CAREERS. Vocational Guidance Manuals, 1971. ($5.75)

THE FIRST NEW ENGLAND CATALOGUE. Chester, Connecticut, The Pequot Press, 1973. ($4.95)
A regional version of the LAST WHOLE EARTH CATALOGUE and the NEW EARTH CATALOGUE. These various catalogues, by the way, are independent of each other from an editorial and publishing standpoint although there is a good deal of resemblance in style and format. The FIRST NEW ENGLAND CATALOGUE notes the following rules for inclusion of an article or item: "(1) It must have a New England address. (2) It must exemplify the idea that New England is not just a place . . . It is a way of life. (3) It must give more than it takes."

Foss, E. W. CONSTRUCTION AND MAINTENANCE FOR FARM AND HOME. Wiley, 1960. ($10.95)

Foster, Catherine O. THE ORGANIC GARDENER. Vintage Books, 1972. ($2.95)
Of the many books that I have read or seen reviewed on gardening by the organic method I like this one best of all and have it in my own library.

THE FOXFIRE BOOK I. Ed. by Eliot Wigginton. Anchor Books, 1972. ($3.95)

THE FOXFIRE BOOK II. Ed. by Eliot Wigginton, Anchor Books, 1973. ($4.95)

Here are remarkable collections of old-time skills and crafts carefully explained and well illustrated. From the South, but quite generally applicable in other regions as well.

Garden Way Publishing. Charlotte, Vermont 05445.
"We, at Garden Way, are truly concerned about the decline in the quality of life both for mankind and for the environment. We are dedicated to the concept of the Garden Way of living — a concept which stresses self-reliance for all individuals and is based on the proposition that the more families who have large vegetable and fruit gardens, the better they, their communities, their nations, and the world will be able to solve the environmental, economic and social problems of our time.
Garden Way Publishing Company's purpose is to help those already involved in gardening and homesteading activities, and also to encourage and guide many more people through the beginning steps. To do this we review literally thousands of books on gardening, country living, and other related activities, and then recommend only those we think most suitable for Garden Wayers. In addition, we publish our own books in areas where we see a definite need, and little suitable material already available.
We are not just another publishing company. We are a company with a particular philosophy, with a specialized purpose, and with a genuine desire to make a positive contribution to the world we all share." Write for the free catalog of books and pamphlets.

Gibbons, Euell. STALKING THE HEALTHFUL HERBS. McKay, 1966.
Not as good as the next book in my list, but well worth reading carefully.

Gibbons, Euell. STALKING THE WILD ASPARAGUS. McKay, 1962.
A superb book that opens our eyes to a whole world of edible food growing wild in the fields and forests, often right at our doorstep. Not only does Mr. Gibbons give excellent directions for identifying the plants, but he also — and this is where his book is better than others — tells how to prepare the plants for the table. I can recommend this book from my own experience.

Goodman, Paul. PEOPLE OR PERSONNEL. Bound with, LIKE
    A CONQUERED PROVINCE. Vintage Books, ($1.95)
This book comes recommended from the Nearings, whose scholarship is beyond reproach. Goodman, who wrote the introduction to
the Nearings' LIVING THE GOOD LIFE says, "I try to show that
the same principles of small-scale operation without cash accounting and managed by the producers themselves can be applied to
many enterprises other than family farming; such enterprises are
often more efficient and productive of real goods, and give far
more security and life-satisfaction, than the centralized, over-
planned, and regimenting mercantilism that is now the pervasive
economic style."

Gourlie, John. HOW TO LOCATE IN THE COUNTRY. Garden
    Way Publishing, 1973. ($3.00)
Advice for the prospective country dweller on how to find where
it's still pleasant in the U.S.

Guise, Cedric C. MANAGEMENT OF FARM WOODLANDS.
    2nd ed. McGraw, 1950. ($11.30)

"Have More" Plan. First published in the nineteen-forties as a
    series conceived by Ed and Carolyn Robinson. Garden Way
    Publishing Co. ($2.50)
The articles were written by leading experts. Garden Way has re-
issued the series because the demand remains strong for these
reports on a variety of gardening and homesteading subjects.

Holstrom, J. G. MODERN BLACKSMITHING. Drake Publica-
    tions, 1971. ($4.95)

Holtrop, W. F. MODERN MACHINE WOODWORKING. Bruce
    Publishing Co., 1960. ($5.88)

Kains, M. G. FIVE ACRES AND INDEPENDENCE: A PRACTI-
    CAL GUIDE TO THE SELECTION AND MANAGEMENT
    OF A SMALL FARM. Greenberg, 1935. Reprinted by Dover
    in 1973. ($2.50)
The Dover Publishing Co. says that, "Generation after generation
has turned to this book as a reliable guide. This is the classic of the

back to the land movement." Kains has excellent advice to offer to people who wish to earn a living from a small farm.

Kaysing, William. HOW TO LIVE IN THE NEW AMERICA. Prentice-Hall, 1972. ($8.95)
Generally written from an anti-Establishment point of view and intended for readers who do not subscribe to conventional socio-economic and philosophical standards. Quite informative over a wide range of topics and certainly very interesting.

Kephart, Horace. CAMPING AND WOODCRAFT: A HAND-BOOK FOR VACATION CAMPERS AND FOR TRAVEL-LERS IN THE WILDERNESS. Macmillan, 1917. ($4.90)
When Kephart said in the sub-title that this is a handbook for vacation campers he had no inkling that there would be such an armada of motorized campers on the highways. He has nothing to say on this subject, but look at the publication date. For the pedestrian camper, he has much to say after even twenty-seven printings. I often read this book, not so much for information about camping and woodcraft techniques, but for a nostalgic look at days that are gone forever. Where Kephart used to glide silently through the woods now a supermarket parking lot cased in asphalt probably is located.

King, Franklin H. FARMERS OF FORTY CENTURIES: OR PERMANENT AGRICULTURE IN CHINA, KOREA AND JAPAN. Rodale Press, Emmaus, Pa. ($7.95)
Long out of print, since its 1911 publication, this excellent work shows how underdeveloped the Western nations are in agriculture compared to the Orient. Read this book. You will find it a real eye-opener.

LAST WHOLE EARTH CATALOG. Edited by Stewart Brand. Random House, 1971. ($5.00)
"The WHOLE EARTH CATALOG functions as an evaluation and access device. With it, the user should know better what is worth getting and where and how to do the getting. An item is listed in the catalog if it is deemed: useful as a tool, relevant to independent education, high quality or low cost, easily available by mail." Others have taken over where the LAST WHOLE EARTH

CATALOG left off. See my references to the FIRST NEW ENG-
LAND CATALOGUE and the NEW EARTH CATALOGUE. All
of these publications have merit and deserve your close attention.

Logsdon, Gene. TWO ACRE EDEN. Paperback Library, 1971.
    ($1.25)

Manwill, Marion C. HOW TO SHOE A HORSE. illus. A. S. Barnes,
    1968. ($4.50)

Martin, John D. THE HOME INCOME GUIDE: OVER 600
    WAYS TO MAKE MONEY AT HOME. Vocational Educa-
    tional Enterprises, 1969. $4.95.
A wide variety of home business activities to choose from, some of
which seem wildly improbable. Yet the author claims that, "each
and every home money-making plan is based either on the author's
own experience, personal observation, or on information which he
believes to be completely reliable."

Martyn, Sean. HOW TO START AND RUN A SUCCESSFUL
    MAIL ORDER BUSINESS. McKay, 1969. ($5.95)
Although I don't particularly care for the mountain of junk mail
the mail order business generates, I'll have to admit that the author
does a good job of patiently explaining how to get started in mail
order.

Monroe, Ruth. KITCHEN CANDLECRAFTING. Barnes, 1970.
    ($6.95)
The author points out, "Many retirees, housewives — even partially
handicapped persons — supplement their income with candles made
in their kitchens. Some of these people have built up an excellent
home candle business with no more talent, time, or ingenuity than
you have."

Moral, Herbert R. BUYING COUNTRY PROPERTY. Garden
    Way Publishing, 1972. ($3.00)
Good advice on what to look for in a country house and how to get
the best mileage out of bankers and real estate dealers.

Morgan, Arthur E. INDUSTRIES FOR SMALL COMMUNITIES,
    WITH CASES FROM YELLOW SPRINGS. Yellow Springs,
    Ohio, Community Service, Inc., 1953.
Arthur Morgan is a recognized expert in community development.
He has been president of Antioch College and chairman of the
Tennessee Valley Authority and from his wide experience he
describes how small industries can thrive in semi-rural areas and
towns.

MOTHER EARTH NEWS. Published bi-monthly. Box 38, Madi-
    son, Ohio 44057.
An excellent magazine for country folk who are not interested in
agribusiness.

Nearing, Helen and Scott. LIVING THE GOOD LIFE: HOW TO
    LIVE SANELY AND SIMPLY IN A TROUBLED WORLD.
    Schocken Books, 1954, 1970.
This classic of country life in the U.S., perhaps is even more
popular now than when it was first published. The Nearings'
ultra-organized life style and ascetic routines and diets may not
appeal to many people. Nevertheless, their sound philosophy, like
that of Henry Thoreau, and their good advice need to be considered
carefully.

Nearing, Helen & Scott. MAPLE SUGAR BOOK: TOGETHER
    WITH REMARKS ON PIONEERING AS A WAY OF LIFE
    IN THE TWENTIETH CENTURY. Schocken Books, 1971
    ($2.75)
The most scholarly work on maple sugar production that I have yet
seen. The Nearings' maple sugar business was their way of making
cash income in the country for a while, and they studied the
economics of this in great detail.

THE NEW EARTH CATALOGUE. G. P. Putnam's Sons, 1973.
    ($4.00)
General in nature and smaller than the LAST WHOLE EARTH
CATALOGUE. Some of the items listed in the NEW EARTH
CATALOGUE may be purchased from them at: P.O. Box 6820
San Francisco, California 94101.

Ogden, Samuel. AMERICA THE VANISHING: RURAL LIFE
    AND THE PRICE OF PROGRESS. Stephen Greene Press,
    1969. ($6.95)

Ogden, Samuel. STEP-BY-STEP TO ORGANIC VEGETABLE
    GROWING. Rodale Press, 1971. ($6.95)

ORGANIC GARDENING AND FARMING. Monthly. Rodale
    Press ($6.85 per year)
I have always enjoyed reading the articles in this magazine.
Skimming through a number of issues always gives some tips on
money-making ventures for country living.

Orwell, George. NINETEEN EIGHTY-FOUR. New American
    Library, 1971 (95¢)
Orwell prophesied the ghastly urban world that is taking shape
around us. Read these grim predictions and then do something
about it.

PUBLISHERS' TRADE LIST ANNUAL. Bowker, 1973. Revised
    annually.
A collection of publishers' catalogs arranged alphabetically by
publishers' names. Bound in several volumes each year, listing
only books in print. A library reference book.

Rand McNally COMMERCIAL ATLAS AND MARKETING
    GUIDE. Rand McNally, 1973. Revised annually.
The best combined source of map and gazetteer data with statistical tables of population, business and manufacturers, agriculture
and other commercial features. Also includes a separate road atlas
of the U.S., Canada and Mexico. A library reference book.

READERS' GUIDE TO PERIODICAL LITERATURE. H. W.
    Wilson Co.
A frequently updated cumulative listing of references to magazine
articles in the most widely circulated English language journals.
This excellent index can be used to find articles by subject, author
and sometimes by title. A library reference work.

Rodale Press. Emmaus, Pennsylvania.
In addition to publishing the monthly periodical, ORGANIC GARDENING AND FARMING, the Rodale Press also has a number of books in print on country life and healthful living. Write for their catalog of publications.

SECOND INCOME NEWS. Monthly. Box 2506 Santa Rosa,
    California 95405. ($12.00 per year)
Lists a large number of income-producing enterprises. A sampling includes speculating in the gold market, recreational aptitude testing, ghost-writing poetry and many hundreds of other unusual ways of making money.

Shirley, Hardy L. FORESTRY AND ITS CAREER OPPORTUNI-
    TIES. 2nd ed. McGraw, 1964. ($12.40)

Small Business Administration. Washington, D.C.
An agency of the U.S. government organized to assist small enterprises with information and loans. Check your phone book for the nearest field office.

Smith, Clodus R. RURAL RECREATION FOR PROFIT. 2nd ed.
    Danville, Illinois, Interstate Printers and Publishers, 1968.
    ($7.25)
This book contains much good information on using country land for recreational purposes.

Smith, Francis G. BEEKEEPING: A BEGINNER'S GUIDE TO
    PROFITABLE HONEY AND BEESWAX PRODUCTION.
    illus. Oxford University Press, 1963. ($3.40)

Sidney, Howard. CAREER OPPORTUNITIES: AGRICULTURAL,
    FORESTRY AND OCEANOGRAPHIC TECHNICIANS AND
    SPECIALISTS. Doubleday. ($11.95)

SUBJECT GUIDE TO BOOKS IN PRINT: AN INDEX TO THE
    PUBLISHERS' TRADE LIST ANNUAL. Bowker, 1973. Re-
    vised annually.
An alphabetical listing by subject of books currently available. A library reference book.

Teilhard de Chardin, Pierre. FUTURE OF MAN. Harper-Row,
    1969. ($1.95)
A more optimistic view than Orwell's and worth reading as a
counterpoint to NINETEEN EIGHTY-FOUR.

THOMAS' REGISTER OF AMERICAN MANUFACTURERS.
    Thomas Publishing Co., 1973. Revised annually.
Arranged by product classifications, list of leading manufacturers,
leading trade names and commercial organizations, chambers of
commerce, boards of trade, etc. General index, product finding
guide to contents and index to advertisers. A library reference work
in several volumes.

Thoreau, Henry D. WALDEN. Doubleday. (95¢)
If you have never read Walden, you should do so immediately. For
Thoreau was one of the most profound thinkers who has yet lived
in the U.S. His philosophy is directly relevant to those who have
read this book.

Towne, Charles W. and Wentworth, E. N. CATTLE AND MEN.
    University of Oklahoma Press, 1955. ($5.95)
A person interested in cattle husbandry would find this historical
book of great interest. It is not a practical manual such as those
publications that can be had from the Extension Service. This book
is about the long and close relationship between cattle and men.

ULRICH'S PERIODICALS DIRECTORY; A CLASSIFIED
    GUIDE TO A SELECTED LIST OF CURRENT PERIODI-
    CALS, FOREIGN AND DOMESTIC. 14th ed. Bowker, 1971-
    72.
More detailed than the Ayer publication given above. An important feature of this library reference work is that it tells where the
periodicals are indexed.

U. S. Department of Agriculture. YEARBOOKS.
These have been published annually for some time. The most
recent one is entitled LANDSCAPE FOR LIVING. As long as the
supply lasts you can get a free copy from your Senator or Congress-
man.

U.S. GOVERNMENT ORGANIZATION MANUAL. Govern-
    ment Printing Office, 1973. Revised annually.

This is the official guide through the maze of Federal bureaucracy. Gives information on the organization, activities (except for the CIA) and current officials of the various departments, offices, commissions, etc. A library reference book.

Vardaman, James M. TREE FARM BUSINESS MANAGEMENT. Ronald Press, 1965. ($7.50)

Virgil. ECLOGUES (or BUCOLICS) and GEORGICS. translated by Thomas Fletcher Royds. Dutton Everyman's Library. ($3.25) The GEORGICS are the great renderings from the Classical world of the joys and hardships of country life. Virgil combines his affection for the rural scene with practical (for his time) advice on tillage, livestock farming, horticulture and beekeeping.

Vocational Education Enterprises. P.O. Box 103. Unionville, Ohio 44088.
Publishers of the HOME INCOME GUIDE and other books and pamphlets on running a business from the home.

Weakley, Tom. HOW TO MAKE CANDLES. Highland Publications, 1971. Distributed by the Stephen Greene Press. ($1.95)

White, E. B. CHARLOTTE'S WEB. Harper-Row, 1952. ($3.95)
Read this for sheer pleasure in the delightful account of country life.

Wilson, Charles M. LET'S TRY BARTER. Devin-Adair, 1960.
The author points out that his book is, "the answer to inflation and the tax collector." Swapping things is a convenient way of getting rid of something you don't need for something you do need and has the advantage that cash money need not enter the picture at all. A thorough study of the intricacies of bartering, as Mr. Wilson has set forth in his book, could be quite advantageous to people who were not brought up in this manner of doing business.

Wright, Austin T. ISLANDIA. New American Library, 1971 ($1.75)
A fascinating fictitious account of the Islandians, their pastoral economy and their successful battle against the inroads of technocracy.

Index